CONTENTS

Get the eBook for free

As a buyer of the printed version of *Crafting a Successful Business*, you can download the electronic version free of charge.

To get hold of your copy of the eBook, simply point your smartphone or tablet camera at this QR code or go to the URL below.

**ebooks.harriman-house.com/
craftingbusiness**

Joanne Dewberry

MY STORY

Hello! My name is Joanne Dewberry – I'm the founder of Charlie Moo's (**www.charliemoos.co.uk**), a craft business that sells handmade party bags and accessories. I live in rural Dorset, with my long-suffering partner David and our three wonderful children Charlie (b. 2007), Megan (b. 2008) and Olive (b. 2011).

When I became pregnant with Charlie I decided to leave my successful career in childcare to raise my family: I could not see the point in looking after other people's children while someone else was looking after mine. But six months in I was bored and missed the mental stimulation my managerial role had given me.

Through our local toddler group we had made lots of friends and Charlie's social life soon needed its own diary. And I began to notice a continuing theme as we went from party to party. I was disheartened by the party bags that Charlie started to receive. Not only did the items – and the bags themselves – break straightaway, but the contents were often very age-inappropriate. At one party he received near-enough a whole bag of chocolate.

It always became a stressful end to a nice afternoon. Charlie would wander out of the party tightly clutching a plastic bag and we would then fight with him to get rid of the bits he could not have; normally he would be left with a balloon and some bubbles.

I wondered whether other parents felt the same. So whilst I was pregnant with our second child, Megan, I spent the summer selling wooden and traditional party bag fillers at local fêtes and fairs. I gathered valuable market research in order to see if I had a market for phase one of my business idea. I then took the plunge and launched a website after Megan was born in August 2008.

This was phase two, as being home with a baby and a one-year-old I knew fêtes were out of my remit for a while. I became very adept at typing with one finger whilst breast-feeding at 2am. In fact this has become a continual theme as I have written most of this book whilst breast-feeding my youngest daughter, Olive.

Once I knew there was a market for wooden and traditional party bag fillers, I wanted to develop the bags themselves. A crafter made the first 100 for me but these sold so quickly that I knew it made better business sense to make them myself. After a shaky start I am now proud to send *my* handmade bags out to my customers.

Phase three is still very much in the pipeline and that will see my award-winning fabric bags being manufactured on a larger scale, which is obviously something I cannot do myself. I am keen to keep with my original ethos and ensure all bags are handmade in the UK but it's trickier than you would think. Currently, large-scale manufacturing mostly happens in China and India. But I am a great believer that things will happen as and when the time is right, and – at the moment – I still enjoy making the party bags. Once the enjoyment factor diminishes and it starts to feel more like a chore, I shall push harder to find manufacturing help: a team of UK sewers running our own production line.

As a multi-award-winning business mum, I enjoy sharing my business knowledge and expertise with other small business owners – especially mums. For me, running my own business has been a way to develop new skills, meet new people and still enjoy being a full-time mother. After writing a successful interactive blog for the past year, I knew this book was inside me. I just needed the courage to let it out!

I work around the busy schedule of three small children and running my own business allows this. No one is saying it's easy, but I love the fact that I can take a 'day off' to enjoy a trip to the beach with the children. It may mean that I have to put a few extra hours in once the children are in bed, but it is worth it to know that we have the freedom to be a family. It is hard work: I am the woman hanging out her washing at 9pm. I know my role in life, what my dreams and aspirations are and how I will achieve them. But I am also a happy mum and I would not change that for the world.

Awards and Achievements

- Top 20 Dorset Business Mother of the Year 2012
- #SBS Theo Paphitis 26.2.12
- Finalist Beat Business Mentor Cambridge Business Mums Conference 2012
- Mumprenuer 100 2011
- Langtry Manor Finalist in PR Initiative 2011
- Nominated Best Party Supplier What's On Awards 2011 and 2012
- Finalist Best Use of Media Mumsclub Awards 2010
- Shortlisted Best Business Mum Mumsclub Awards 2010
- Enterprise Nation Ideas 101 Winner June 2010
- Shortlisted Business Parent of the Year – Mums and Working Awards
- Shortlisted in the World Skill Competition 2010 (Networking Mummies)
- Recognised for Very Good Service 2010
- Shortlisted Make Your Mark in the Market 2010
- Winner of Dorset Business Mother of the Year 2010 – Langtry Manor
- Nominated MADS Blog Award 2010, 2011 and 2012
- Langtry Manor Best Green Business Finalist 2010
- TGF Best Rated Award Winner 2009
- Winner of Future 100 Young Entrepreneurs 2009
- Highly Commended MumsClub.co.uk PR Comp 2009

THANKS TO …

So many wonderful people have helped me with writing this book, from all my case studies to all my Facebook fans (**www.facebook.com/joannedewberry.co.uk**) who have answered my questions and given me a great deal to think about; Viv Smith, Nadine Thomas, Laura Renton, Erica Martyn, Jo Fazel, Jamie Fry, Andrea Palluch … I hope I haven't missed anyone!!

Special thanks must go to my parents and brother – so Mum, Dad and David "Special Thanks" to you.

To the Giltrow Gang – David, Charlie, Megan and Olive – it is not always easy being someone's partner and even harder being someone's parent but you guide me through the tough times, and make me smile and super proud through the good times. I love you all very much – *Charlie Moo defo more than a beenana!!*

I feel blessed to have such wonderful friends who have helped me in various ways from technical support to proofreading – Rachel Whitelock, Sam Thewlis, Darren Toms and Heather Martyn. However, there seems to have been heaps of support but no wine … next book please bring wine!!!

To anyone I may have forgotten, it wasn't intentional and I'm sure a signed copy will make things all good!! Phew!

CHAPTER

ONE

WHY CHOOSE CRAFTING?

The UK handmade market is currently riding high as our attitudes to shopping changes. With this comes a new wave of local manufacturers.

Are you are a producer of handmade products and wondering:

- Whether you could turn your hobby into a small business?

- Where to find information on where to sell your products on and offline?

- How to price your products, including wholesale and sale or return options?

- How to develop a unique and recognisable brand that will enable you to stand out from the crowd?

- Where to start with visual merchandising?

- How to use social media to market your business, building up an excellent PR portfolio but spending little or no money?

This book not only takes you through these points in no-nonsense, plain English, but also has quirky craft activities to complete along the way, highlighting hints and tips from real-life crafty small business owners in the know.

I am not naturally crafty – when I started Charlie Moo's in 2008 I had not used a sewing machine since textiles at school – but I soon discovered a love for sewing, and how therapeutic it can be. Along the way I have learnt lots of new business skills which I am passionate about sharing with small business owners, and in particular business mums or 'mumprenuers'. With three children under five myself, I understand the constraints on mums in business. I believe my passion and dedication enabled me to earn the title of Dorset Business Mum of the Year 2010, along with numerous other business accolades in the past few years.

No one can deny the craft market is taking the UK by storm. Arts and crafts is having a huge revival and consumers are increasingly looking for unique, one-off items for themselves, their children or as gifts. People are breaking away from mass-market living; shunning the cloned society where we all dress the same and raise our identically dressed children in our matching houses. Consumers are starting to take more notice of where and how products are made. For years we have found ourselves shopping in out-of-town superstores for our clothing, furniture and food, but in recent times more and more people are breaking away and going back to the high street, looking to support independent local businesses.

 Arts and crafts really are leading the way in recycling, longevity and uniqueness."

Our lifestyle habits are also beginning to go full circle as consumers (and the government) are trying not to be such a throwaway society. For example, seamstresses making keepsake teddies from your child's baby clothes, or pillowcase dresses which will grow with your daughter from dress to top are both incredibly popular. Arts and crafts really are leading the way in recycling, longevity and uniqueness.

When I started Charlie Moo's I never really set out to be a 'crafter' and to be honest I still do not really class myself as one now. This could be because I have steered clear of conventional craft-selling avenues, such as Etsy and MISI, or traditional craft markets. I can sew fabric party bags but that was really born out of necessity.

Really, this is where my craft talent ends. The bulk of my business is handmade party bags and I sell these in large quantities, so I have never looked at increasing my hand-crafted product range; with three children I just would not have the time.

As a small business owner my real talent lies in PR, marketing and developing brand awareness. Making regular appearances on local radio, in local and national newspapers and in magazines has been the driving force, whether that be as Charlie Moo's or as myself discussing small business information and development. I only have television left to conquer!

Along the way I have met some incredibly gifted artists and craftspeople from all manner of disciplines. It has become apparent to me that many of the 'craft' businesses I have spoken to grew from a hobby, often making items for friends, or as gifts; in contrast to my journey where I had to learn a 'hobby' in order to start my business. There is no right or wrong way to start. If you already have a hobby that you are skilled in, you can build on orders from friends and family and grow it that way. Or you can do your research beforehand, find out where there is a gap in the market and learn a skill that fills it.

"Odds & Soxlets began after making various sock monkeys, along with illustrated hand-crafted cards for my friends and family as gifts for birthdays and other special occasions. I had such an amazing response that I decided to launch Odds & Soxlets as my first business venture, so my sock creations and illustrations will be available for all to love and enjoy!"

– Erica Martyn (www.oddsandsoxlets.co.uk)

Whilst researching this book I came across a whole host of craft businesses (and a variety of disciplines, motivations, prices, sales techniques, etc.), enabling me to share with you an incredible wealth of resources.

Here are my pros and cons to starting a craft business.

Pros

● Ultimately, it should be enjoyable.

Emma Ringer (**www.EyeSpyBaby.co.uk**) says, "I am still surprised every time I get an order, because I am getting paid for doing something I love!"

Crafting is a great way to de-stress, relax *and* make money.

● You don't have to stick to one craft. Sewing, knitting, card-making, painting, jewellery-making – there is a wide variety out there.

● Craft businesses generally incur small start-up costs. Even so, you will find that lots of people buy all the equipment and don't use it, so it's worth a trip round your local charity shops and car boot sales to keep those start-up costs minimal.

"You can start slowly and build your business organically without needing major investment."

– Nadine Thomas (www.nellie-dean.com)

● As the products you're making are unique, there's no need for hoards of stock. Customers will be buying each item specifically or you will be making to order.

● It's good for the soul.

"Seeing your ideas come to life – for me, designing an item of clothing that people actually want to buy for their children, then seeing amazing pictures of their little ones wearing it. It honestly makes me smile, even now. It's really very rewarding."

– Laura Renton (www.thatssewlaura.co.uk)

- You choose the products you make and sell, which enables you to continually monitor the market and adjust and adapt accordingly.

- There is a huge variety of channels through which to sell your products, both on and offline, which should cater for your individual needs.

- It's easy to fit around your children and other commitments – many people I have spoken to have been developing their small business around other employment.

  It's also a great way to get your children interested in being creative.

- You don't need to have an extra room to store your equipment or to work from (I used to sew at my dining-room table) but make sure you clear up every single pin (husbands get cross if you don't!).

- You are your own boss, so you can pick and choose your hours, how and when you work, how and where you sell your products, the orders you take on and what price to charge.

  You can run your business exactly how you want – you're not answerable to anyone.

Cons

- Income is variable and irregular.

- It takes a lot of effort to get your name 'out there' – especially when you probably just want to be creating products.

- When you first start up there is you and only you. YOU are jack-of-all-trades; photographer, accountant, PR, sales, customer services, tea maker, etc. It can be incredibly hard being spread so thinly, especially if your products are time-consuming to make. However, they are all necessary parts of making your business successful.

- You can get lost amongst other crafters, especially on websites such as Etsy or MISI.

- Competing products produced in factories can be made at a fraction of the price, so stay clear of the obvious and think unique, kitsch and limited edition.

- It can be lonely working from home. Make sure you join business networking groups to learn new skills and meet other small business owners. Also think about attending craft coffee mornings, enabling you to network with fellow crafters. If you can't find one, then start your own!

- You can easily be distracted by people, the telephone, social networking, cleaning, etc. Procrastination is easily succumbed to when working from home.

- Margins can be low, therefore make sure you have a good pricing formula and that you know the cost of all your materials. Also, ensure you factor in the cost of your time.

- Paperwork can be vast for a small business! For example, handmade toys require a CE mark. You are responsible for knowing the relevant laws.

- Many of the crafters I have interviewed made the same point about having their creative license copied as soon as their product is 'out there'. Unfortunately, those tools which enable you to promote your business online can be your downfall too. When your products are selling well you inevitably open yourself up to being easily copied.

- You can lose motivation, passion and interest.

Turning a hobby into a business has a huge learning curve. I believe that to be successful you need to have had experience in all the key areas and know the ins and outs of how the whole business fits together.

WHAT SKILLS DO YOU NEED?

Many people I spoke to had been taught crafting skills by family members such as mothers and grandmothers. I do think you need to have a degree of creative flair, passion and interest – as well as patience! – to turn a hobby or new skill into a successful business. Skill-wise, there are so many 'How To ...' books out there that you can pretty much learn to do anything. Save your start-up capital by borrowing books from the library, buying second-hand books, reading blogs about crafting or watching 'How To...' videos on YouTube. And remember: practice will make you better. My first few party bags were awful but I soon learnt what worked and, just as importantly, what didn't. I used old clothing and pillowcases to develop my technique rather than spending money on new fabrics. Keep in mind ways you can cut back on spending money in the beginning.

If you want to do more formal training there are plenty of courses available. Try your local adult learning centre, where you will find a variety of craft courses, such as sewing (how to use your machine and how to make specific items), painting and drawing, jewellery-making and upholstering furniture. They are normally day courses, over a weekend, or short courses of a few hours a week for six weeks or so. They are generally between £50 and £100 (however if you receive various benefits you can get the courses at a reduced rate and sometimes even free but you will need to check at your local adult learning centre). For sewing courses, check out your local haberdashery shop if you're looking to develop skills or learn how to use your machine correctly. These can cost around £25 to £40, excluding materials.

Andrea Palluch (**www.skinbistro.co.uk**) used Google and word of mouth to secure the training she required:

> "I found all my skincare courses online after years of searching. They were around £150 per day. I gained my Diploma in Aromatherapy from a course recommended to me by an

aromatherapist I met on one of the skincare courses. In total, including anatomy and physiology and five days in the South of France, the cost was around £3500."

Course prices vary depending on who is running them, where they are located and whether there is a qualification or a new skill to gain. Do your research and ask other local crafters whether they did any training, and if so where. If your start-up capital is very small you could always arrange sessions at your home. Invite other crafters along, share skills and techniques and try new things.

I believe that when starting a small crafting business, the pros outweight the cons. It can entail a lot of hard work to promote but that's really no different to any other business. However, if you are also making products then your day-to-day running time is much more limited. If you are serious about moving from hobby to profitable business there is a lot to consider. Let's get started.

ACTIVITY #1:
HANDMADE CARD

by Erica Martyn (**oddsandsoxlets.co.uk**)

You will need

- A computer and printer

- Card stock/paper/tall card blank

- Odds & Soxlets 'Toots' Digi Stamp Collection – two patterned papers, character and sentiment digi stamps

- Colouring pencils and ink pad

- Adhesives and cutting tools

- Strips of white and pink ribbon
- Sticky pink gemstones

Method

Step 1. Email: ericamartyn@oddsandsoxlets.co.uk using the code JDCSSB-TOOTS to receive a FREE Toots Sock Monkey Digi Stamp.

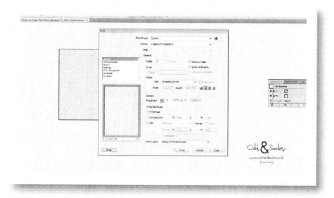

Step 2. Extract all of the elements from your digital file and print to your desired sized. Print both patterned papers onto basic, plain, A4 white paper.

11

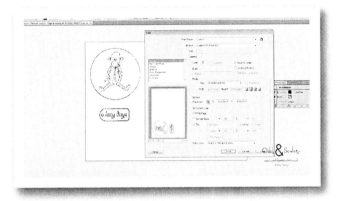

Resize the character digi and fit into a circular shape as a cutting guide, then place the sentiment below to the required size using whatever software you have available and print onto basic plain white card.

Step 3. Once you have printed all your elements, collect together all the things you will need and find a suitable table/desk space to make your project.

Step 4. Cut out the spotty patterned paper to fit your card blank. Cut the pink polka dot paper into a strip to run across the middle. Cut your character digi around the circle template and cut out your sentiment tag.

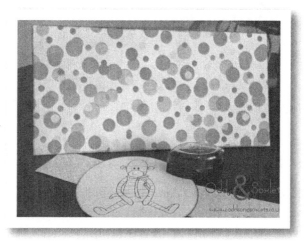

Step 5. Adhere the spotty paper to the card blank and using your ink pad ink the edges of the front of the card and around your polka dot strip and circular character to give them a rough coloured edge.

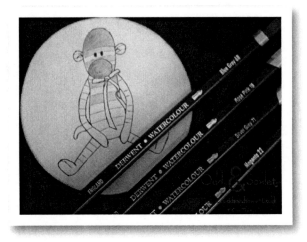

Step 6. Colour your digi stamp character using coloured pencils.

Step 7. Adhere your polka dot strip across the centre of your card. Cut two lengths of ribbon slightly larger than the length of the card, adhere them to the centre of the card along the length of the polka dot strip. Punch a hole in the sentiment tag and thread ribbon through. Add 3D foam squares to the back of the character digi circle and sentiment tag.

Step 8. Adhere onto the card as shown and add three sticky pink gemstones to the left of the tag.

© Erica Martyn, **www.oddsandsoxlets.co.uk**

CHAPTER
TWO

IS THE PRICE RIGHT?

Pricing your products right is vital. You don't want to pitch too low and risk not making a profit, but at the same time you don't want to go too high and price yourself out of the market. You will find that some crafters sell their creations extremely cheap in comparison to your well thought out prices, either because they are not registered as a business and do this for pocket money, or they have not got a clue about pricing. This can make it harder for those who play by the rules and, more importantly, know their product's value. Do not be lured into lowering your prices – remember you are crafting a successful small business.

 Pricing your products right is vital."

You need to know these three key prices for each of your products. This is where your business success will lie.

1. **Cost price** – this is the **actual cost** for you to make each piece, including time, overheads, raw materials, etc.

2. **Trade price** – this is the price you're willing to **sell to stockists** and enable you to still make a profit.

3. **Retail price** – as a general rule the retail price should be **twice the trade price**. If you do sell to stockists – whether that be via wholesale or 'sale or return' (we will come back to these terms later in Chapter Four) – stick to this retail price as you do not want to undercut your stockists.

Make sure you know these three prices off by heart, or if not then always have them to hand. It will make you look far more professional if you are asked unexpectedly. Also make sure you review them on a regular basis, and think about the elements which may change, such as the minimum wage or the price of raw materials. You do not want to suddenly find you are only breaking even, or worse still making a loss.

WORKING OUT YOUR COST PRICE

My advice is to devise a simple formula. The figures you need to include and consider are: your time, the cost of raw materials, and what others are charging for similar products. I think this is the fairest way to develop a pricing scheme.

Example

This is a *very* basic example to give you the general idea.

Cost of supplies per unit

If a metre of material is £2.50 and that is enough to make eight bags then the unit price is 31p (£2.50 ÷ 8 = £0.31).

I buy all my cotton, labels, swing tags and string in bulk, which per item costs less than 1p, so I add 5p to each bag, which brings the total to 36p.

£0.31 + £0.05 = £0.36

Your time

You want to earn £6.08 per hour (the minimum wage in 2012) and can make five bags per hour, so each one costs you £1.22 in labour (£6.08 ÷ 5 = £1.22).

The competition

I would take the average price from three similar businesses. For example, A = £1.99, B = £1.49, C = £2.00, so the average is £1.83 ([£1.99 + £1.49 + £2.00] ÷ 3 = £1.83).

The break-even point is £1.58 (36p + £1.22), meaning any money made above that is profit, and your competitors' average selling price is £1.83. Taking all this into consideration I would look at your recommended retail price (RRP) being between £1.85 and £2.

If you make more substantial items such as jewellery, paintings or clay hand casts, then Viv Smith's (**www.poppysparkles.co.uk**) formula would work better for you:

> "I have a formula – although I do occasionally tweak it if I feel something is coming out too pricey and just won't sell: materials + time + overheads. I then add 20% and then double it. This means that I have priced in a way that enables me to do trade and retail without making a loss. I see so many handmade items priced in such a way that it's not even a self-funding hobby! I won't compete on price – I'm working on building a strong brand and offering a great shopping experience."

Things to take into consideration:

- You ideally want to pay yourself NO LESS than minimum wage.

Rates from 1 October 2011

The national minimum wage rates are reviewed each year by the Low Pay Commission. As of 1 October 2011:

- the main rate for workers aged 21 is £6.08 (rising to £6.19 in October 2012)

- the 18–20 rate is £4.98

- the 16–17 rate for workers above school leaving age but under 18 is £3.68

- the apprentice rate, for apprentices under 19 or 19 or over and in the first year of their apprenticeship is £2.60 (rising to £2.65 in October 2012).

  (*This information is taken from* **www.direct.gov.uk**. *Check the new rates every October and increase your prices accordingly.*)

- When calculating your cost price, do factor in waste, shipping, equipment and advertising, as well as utilities such as broadband, electricity and calls. You will probably need to make an educated guess for this.

- Weigh up your target market. High-end clients will expect to pay a premium for handmade products.

- Do not pitch yourself too low. When the orders start flying in and you are up at all hours making products and the cash tin is empty, you will struggle to raise your prices and keep the orders coming.

Be reasonably competitive but DO NOT compete on price. Your products will inevitably vary from those of your competitors as they have been handmade by two completely different people. Competing on price is never going to be sustainable – it is also very poor practice and not an ideal business model. It can only lead to failure in the end (unless you are selling vast numbers of units and benefitting from large economies of scale). For handmade businesses, your USP (unique selling point) is that each item has been made by you and not mass-produced. Your prices also reflect the standard of your product. If you price too low, customers will not have confidence that your product is well made.

A crafter's most valuable resource is their time; some may have more than others, but ultimately this is what prices your products at a premium. If you're going to give your time away for free then you will not develop a successful business. Instead of seeking to lower your product prices in order to compete with others, look at your USP. Think of ways in which you can develop a strong brand, ensuring potential customers will want to do business with you even if you are not the cheapest on the market. Jamie Fry (**www.creativestores.co.uk/UncleBundleCrafts**) describes below how he used to be guilty of underselling himself and his products:

> "I used to do my research online and try to fit in with those prices or lower, but would never make any money. Also, initially I was buying my materials from high street stores but soon realised that I needed to get myself some trade accounts to buy wholesale. I do, however, have an individual price for every part of a make and at the moment simply round it up to a sensible selling price."

Jamie has already started to make the necessary changes to increase his profitability. His next step is to construct a pricing formula which works for him and his customer base.

* * *

When I posed the question "How do you decide on price/ monetise your products?" to a variety of different craft businesses, the response was varied.

Michelle Williams (**www.craftecademy.co.uk**) agreed with my suggestion to have a formula:

> "Taking into account all of the costs; not only the cost of the materials, but also make sure you factor in your time accordingly! Remember, when people are buying hand-crafted goods, they are paying for your time. Many handmade goods take a considerable amount of time to make, not to mention skill and dedication! Many people sell their craft products at a price that is too low when you actually analyse the amount of time that has gone into making them. Always check out your competitors too, to see what their pricing strategy is and position against them appropriately."

Michelle also points out that your pricing strategy should be appropriate to your target market too. It's important to think about who you are targeting and where you will sell your products, as this will have also have a bearing on your pricing.

Caroline Watts (**www.carolinewattsembroidery.co.uk**) gives a prime example of how she tailors her prices and products to her target market, dependent on where, when and how she is selling:

> "Pricing for me depends on where my products will be sold; for local craft fairs I have to charge less than I would online. It is very much pricing for the market you sell in. I don't sell my current range at craft fairs because in Yorkshire people don't seem to be prepared to pay full price but if it is a bargain they are likely to buy a few small things. At craft fairs I tend to sell samples, seconds and end of line products."

However, some crafters said that they like to try and keep their product pricing more 'real':

> "I often think 'what would I pay for this?' My prices have changed over the years. I can now get more for my work because I have built up a reputation and of course my skills keep improving. I do believe though that crafters cannot charge for the time and effort that goes into their lovely things, and so we at best accept a reasonable donation, and I am happy with that."
>
> **– Catherine L Owen, The Raggy Rat**
> **(www.facebook.com/raggyrat)**

In my opinion these people are not interested in developing a brand or a business, they are looking for a hobby whereby they can make a few pennies if that.

Costing correctly is vital to the success of your business so take the time in the beginning to develop a formula and get to grips with your pricing.

N.B.

I'm not going to cover keeping accounts, cash flow, VAT, etc. in this book as there are literally hundreds of existing books that already do that.

ACTIVITY #2:
FRESH FACE MASK

by Skin Bistro (www.skinbistro.co.uk)

This is a simple recipe which you can make with ingredients bought at the supermarket.

You can choose from a variety of fruits, dairy or tea as the 'liquid' part and for the 'dry' part there is cocoa powder through to clay. It's always good to pick your ingredients according to your skin type.

If you don't use the whole preparation in one treatment, keep the rest in the fridge and use within three days.

- Liquid part: 2 teaspoons
- Dry part: 1 teaspoon

Recipes

Skin Type	Liquid Part	Dry Part
Dry or mature skin	Mashed avocado, double cream	Cocoa powder
Sensitive	Grape juice or pulp, yoghurt	Ground oats
Combination, blemished, oily	Peppermint tea, mashed raspberry	Green clay, rice flour

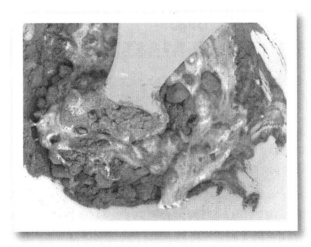

Step 1. Mix both ingredients together until you get a smooth paste consistency. Apply to your clean, dry face. You can use the back of your mixing teaspoon to smooth the liquid onto your face. This works really well!

Step 2. Leave it for 10–15 minutes, until it's dry. If you have dry or sensitive skin, leave it for less time (5–10 minutes), just so that the mask doesn't dry on your face.

Step 3. To rinse it off, wet a face cloth with tepid water, wring it out lightly, stretch it and press it gently against your face. Leave it for one minute and then wipe the mask off. Rinse the cloth and repeat until the mask is completely removed. To finish off, splash your face with cold water.

Honey is a versatile addition to your mask and can be used for any skin type. If you suffer from blemishes or spots, Manuka honey may help alleviate the condition. Add 1/2 teaspoon to any of the recipes above.

© Skin Bistro UK

CHAPTER

THREE

BRANDING

The key to branding is to consider every aspect of your business, including yourself. Ensure you work with colours, styles and themes which you can easily use over the various aspects of your business consistently, especially if you market via social media such as Twitter and Facebook and/or if you intend to sell at craft fairs.

"I restrict my headers, blog, logo, labels, etc. to three main colours of red, aqua and white and two fonts. This ensures that there is cohesion across all promotional material and will help lead towards brand recognition."

– Nadine Thomas (www.nellie-dean.com)

Business branding does not start and end with a fabulous logo. Branding needs to encompass your whole business, including your ethos, core values and mission statement. Ultimately, when a customer sees your brand, what key things do you want to spring to mind?

 Business branding does not start and end with a fabulous logo."

The name 'Charlie Moo's' developed from my son – Charlie. We have referred to him as "Moo" since he was a baby. Obviously Moo lends itself quite nicely to the cow imagery. My friend came up with the concept of the cow being the letter M and it works on so many levels:

- As a full banner using the whole name or just using the M cow as a stand-alone logo, which does not look out of place and is still distinctly Charlie Moo's.

- The style of the M cow also lends itself nicely to being transformed into both my girl cows, Megan and Olive. Megan Moo is a flip of Charlie, so is facing in the opposite direction and brown and pink in colour. Olive Moo is a mix of the brown and black of the Charlie and Megan cows and as my own quirk has olive-green accessories.

● These stand-alone cow images work well as images on cake toppers, my popular range of wrapping paper and other products.

For the Royal Wedding in April 2011, I used Charlie and Megan Moo adorned with crowns on a backdrop of the Union Jack. For Easter I have them wearing bunny masks. All quirky, unique and distinctly Charlie Moo's. This enables me to keep my branding consistent but also topical, seasonal and fresh.

I also ensure that each bag I make has a label sewn inside it, a swing tag attached to the handle with string made from an image of one of our party bags, and I pop a business card inside too. That way, each child that leaves a party with one of my handmade fabric bags – or, perhaps more importantly, their parents – knows where the bag came from.

Charlie Moo's branding has been designed to reflect our:

● unique, fun and funky approach

● good value

● excellent customer service.

What you need to ask yourself when developing a brand for your business is:

1. Who am I?

2. What image do I want to portray? Am I professional, trendy, quirky, modern, etc.?

3. What do I want to deliver?

4. Who is my target market? My ideal client? What drives them? What are their aspirations? What are their needs?

5. What is my USP? What is my niche?

6. What is my business personality and how can I convey that to potential customers?

7. Who is my competition?

8. What is my strapline and will people know what I do from it?

That's Sew Laura has the strapline 'Taking over the world ... one child's wardrobe at a time!' Instantly you know that the products they sew are children's clothing.

Branding questions

1. Who am I?

My name is Jo. I am a mother of two gorgeous little girls and business owner of **www.bestbabyshower.co.uk**.

2. What image do I want to portray?

I want to be seen as highly professional, offering a great choice of beautiful and quality products and absolutely focused on fabulous customer service.

3. What do I want to deliver?

I strive to be able to offer my customers the widest choice of baby shower party supplies and gifts in the UK. I always aim to offer something a little bit different and constantly expand my product catalogue so that my customers can find everything they need to host a brilliant baby shower all in one place.

4. Who is my target market?

My target market is mainly women between the ages of 18 and 35. Some may be pregnant, but many will be the friends and family members of pregnant women. Most customers will be responsible for hosting a baby shower for someone else, which can be a daunting task. I aim to help make it easier by:

- Keeping the costs down for them by offering fairly priced products, plus a price match guarantee and offering discounts to my newsletter subscribers, social media fans and advert readers.

- Acknowledging that often customers leave it late to order items for the party (and helping by having a fast dispatch time and using first class post (or couriers where necessary), enabling customers to request priority dispatch where possible, and offering downloadable baby shower games which don't require physical shipping.

- Realising that customers like handmade, personalised and unique products and ensuring that I offer a large choice of these items.

- Making it easy for customers to find what they are looking for by having a clear and user-friendly website with easy navigation.

- Helping with ideas by offering a free baby shower guide full of planning hints, checklists and ideas for themes, venues, food and games.

5. What makes me special?

I strive to ensure my customer service is second to none. As someone who often makes purchases online myself I am frequently shocked by the often poor customer service I have received by larger and more well known companies. Each customer is equally important, whether they have spent £1 or £100, and I treat them as such. I dispatch items within the time-scales I set out, I answer queries when I say I will, and I always go the extra mile to make sure that my customers get their items on time and are delighted with them. Baby showers are still a niche area in the UK, although they are becoming more and more popular. I understand that each and every order is important because the items are needed to throw a very special day for a special pregnant lady or to congratulate a couple on the arrival of a new life. As a mother myself I understand how much it means.

6. What is my business personality?

I always aim to come across as professional at all times. Although I do use social media such as Twitter and Facebook to engage with customers and potential customers, I always ensure that I am careful with what I write. I don't get involved in arguments, swear or generally give the impression that I am anything other than professional. On the telephone I am always courteous and helpful – even to marketeers and cold callers – as I never know who may need my services in the future (I am sure I will stand out positively in their minds compared to the 100 other businesses who put the phone down on them or are rude). I  am the business and the business is me, so I have to think with my business head on at all times.

7. Who are my competition?

I have two main online competitors and I make sure that I know what changes they may be making or how they are fairing in the search engine rankings. My competitive streak drives me to ensure that I am always striving to be the best at what I do.

8. What is my strapline?

I don't have a strapline as such on my website as my business name is fairly stand-alone, however I would sum it up as 'Beautiful Baby Shower Party Supplies & Gorgeous Gifts'.

> **N.B.**
>
> For more businesses that have answered these questions please see the Case Studies section. It is useful to see the questions, answers and the business' final logo.

You need to take all aspects of the design into consideration; fonts, colours, and how the logo will work alongside your existing designs or packaging.

This is an important aspect of your business so if you're not a graphic designer then employ somebody to help you. The original Charlie Moo's logo was designed in the basic MS Paint program and was incredibly square and pixellated. A graphic designer smoothed it all out and made it more visually appealing, which instantly changed the whole appearance of my website and has since paved the way for Megan and Olive Moo. These high-quality images can then also be easily used on branded items such as wrapping paper and cake toppers.

FONTS

The font you choose is crucial to the feel of your brand. If you are going for funky, fun and child-friendly then you don't want to pick something like Times New Roman. Instead, you might possibly choose something friendlier like Comic Sans MS, which is used a lot by teachers.

It's useful to try a few styles. Different fonts suggest different things, and experimenting is the best way to get it right.

 The font you choose is crucial to the feel of your brand."

Try to be unique and interesting at the same time as you aim for a style that reflects your products, personality *and* target market. But do bear in mind readability for potential customers. Your font also needs to fit in with your logo if you choose to have one. For example, Charlie Moo's font needed to be bold, black and plain to ensure it did not detract from the cow-shaped M.

"I like the font to 'translate' the feeling of what the business is about so mine are bright and in a handwritten style."

– Monica Strydom (www.myfunnybunny.com)

"I like to use Arial Rounded a lot; it's simple with a childish feel without being a kids' handwriting font."

– Zara Russell (www.cutezie-poo.com)

COLOURS

Take your time when deciding on your brand colours. Find out what emotions and connotations a colour conjures up. For example, red is the colour of fire and blood, evoking associations with energy, war, danger, strength, power and determination, as well as passion, desire, and love. Whereas green is calming and nurturing. Consider the kind of feeling you want associated with your business.

> "Purple is psychologically attached to creativity, and gold to high quality."
>
> **– Julie Morrisroe (www.facebook.com/groups/chameleonesque)**

Once you have decided on your colour(s) ensure that you carry them throughout your business image and branding. Viv Smith (**www.poppysparkles.co.uk**) notes how important this is to your image:

> "To provide a stylish, cohesive look to my website and all other business items, I use colours picked from my logo, along with grey for the wordy bits for ease of reading and to avoid an attack of the pinks."

Take the time to match your colour palette exactly by finding out the specific name or number for each colour. If you design yourself then you will already know this, but if you use a designer make sure you ask them. Your website, business cards and packaging will be more consistent and distinctive.

PACKAGING

The majority of the time your packaged items will be many customers' first physical encounter with your business, whether through the post or on display at a fair. So, is the packaging essential? Yes. Packaging plays a major role in your brand (and repeat custom) but it does not have to be expensive or elaborate.

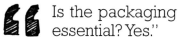 Is the packaging essential? Yes."

Choose packaging that reflects your business. If you promote your green credentials then look at using recycled paper, a more rustic feel, biodegradable items or even recycled envelopes. I do this with Charlie Moo's, then I brand them with my stickers and labelling. I also state this on my website so that customers are aware.

Your packaging does not have to be expensive but some careful thought can have a really positive effect on your customers' experience. Think about simple ideas, like gift-wrapping products in tissue paper and ribbon in co-ordinating colours that match your branding. This is not only cost-effective but will also look effortlessly beautiful. A handwritten note is guaranteed to make your customer feel positive towards your business and enhance the feel-good factor of their shopping experience with you.

"I think good packaging has a huge part to play in repeat custom. If you're not getting the chance to represent the business face to face, your packaging is the first thing they see, so it needs to sell the business and make customers want to receive it again... If not they might not remember you."

– Laura Renton (www.thatssewlaura.co.uk)

"I will not be the only person who upon seeing some gorgeous packaging eye-candy, such as the Boux Avenue gift bags, feel jealousy wash over me and wish it was me that was carrying a luxurious gift bag – that's the power of well branded packaging. It evokes positive emotions in the recipient and makes others covet it."

–Viv Smith (www.poppysparkles.co.uk)

Take a minute now to think about what you want your packaging to say about your business. If you already have some, does it tick all the boxes and answer all the questions you asked yourself at the beginning?

- Who am I?

- What image do I want to portray?

- What do I want to deliver?

- Who are my target market?

- What makes me special?

- What is my business personality?

- Who are my competition?

- What is my strapline?

REPETITION

Repetition is a useful branding tool. There is no point having an excellent logo/brand image if you do not utilise it. As mentioned before, when I send out an order, each party bag has a label sewn on the inside with the website address on it (**www.charliemoos.co.uk**). The bags also have a hanging label attached to the handle, on which is my website address and a lovely image of a fabric party bag in use. I place a business card inside each bag too.

Depending on what else is being sent with the bags, I also have an array of Charlie Moo's branded stickers. Once the party bags have been handed out to all the children, bits can get lost or ruined but I have covered all bases to enable their parents (who are now potential new customers) to find Charlie Moo's. Although, having a unique and quirky name helps too.

You should also continue this repetition across your online presence. Ensure you are using the same imagery on all your social media sites, website, blog, etc. This keeps you easily identifiable to existing and potential customers and enables your business to stand out from any competitors. In addition, make sure you are using the same 'voice' in your tweets, Facebook page status and blog posts.

Developing a credible brand is just as important as the look and feel. Encourage customers to leave feedback on your website, shop, Facebook page (review tabs can easily be added to a page) etc., whether that is for the products themselves or the service they received. Potential customers will appreciate this. You can encourage customers to leave feedback/testimonials/reviews by placing a card in with their order, a 'review this' link in their dispatch email and a dedicated follow-up email a week or two afterwards. And you can always remind customers via social media too.

PERSONAL BRANDING

When representing your business, consider the image that *you* convey. This not only includes your appearance – think personal visual merchandising – but also how you represent yourself as your brand and how you come across online. This is as important to the customer as what you are actually selling.

When selling at events you probably routinely organise banners, table cloths and visual merchandising props, but do not forget to purchase or make yourself a uniform. A branded t-shirt and/or name badge, handmade branded money belt or even an apron adorned with your logo and in your business colours would work well. These items enable you to stand out from other exhibitors and reinforce the brand, helping to make it instantly recognisable. People buy from people, so your appearance, as well as your personality and passion for your products/business, is even more on show when you sell at fêtes, fairs, etc. Make it count. Develop relationships and make yourself as well known as your products and branding. Every encounter is a possible sale.

Jamie Fry (**www.creativestores.co.uk/UncleBundleCrafts**) is all too familiar with ensuring he represents himself correctly. *He is his USP:*

> "At fêtes and fairs some people can't believe what they are seeing (I am bald and have a few tattoos – only visible on a sunny day!). When I am with my wife, or when my mother or sister help out, they get all the compliments, and when they tell them it was all me some just say 'Yeah, right,' laugh and walk on, and others are like 'Wow, really, that's so cool'. That's my USP."

A good personal image does wonders for your brand.

Active social media enables you to gain a following and gather momentum, which in turn drives potential customers to your website and events. Think about how you come across in terms of your tone, your language and your message. Take into consideration everything you say and how this could affect the brand you are developing. Some comments are simply not professional. If you have had a bad day with your children or an argument with your husband you only cheapen yourself and your brand by using a public forum to vent this. This also goes for any awkward or unhappy customers that have wound you up. Do not complain about them. Do not use social media to manifest your frustrations; tell your other half, or the wall, but not the world. On the other hand, if a customer uses social media to complain about your business

 It is the overall experience that your consumer is looking for."

or customer service ensure you reply straightaway. It's not all about damage limitation, it is also about making sure *you* value your brand and your customers and that others can see that.

How you represent yourself says a lot about your brand and reflects the kind of service your customers will receive. Your attention to detail will always pay dividends in the end. Remember, it is the overall experience that your consumer is looking for and judging. You may think that those added extras go unnoticed – the personal touch, the branded image, the little quirks – but they should come together to create a desirable brand that translates into sales.

TO SUM UP

Before you spend any money on logos, business cards, leaflets, web design, etc., it is really useful to get other people's opinion. Try to avoid *just* asking family members as they will have a tendency to give a positive appraisal rather than the constructive criticism you need. Developing a brand is not an easy process, but once it is right you've then got to reinforce it in everything you say and do. It inevitably encompasses everything about you and what your business does.

"Our logo and branding suggests clean, simple, natural and fresh, both with the colours and daisy image. We used simple lines and colours to help portray this. Initially we had lots of potential logos and looked at them all side by side and in the context of an advert to help choose the final one. We also checked that they looked OK in black and white and grey scale."

– Rose Glendinning (www.nappybliss.co.uk)

"When it came to branding my site I knew generally speaking that an online shop selling baby-related items would need to look 'cute' but also professional. I didn't want really bright colours but rather more muted, classy tones that immediately make people think 'baby'. So it seemed ideal to use baby blues, pinks and neutral beige as they work so well together. When I first started out I had a logo designed by a friend, which I decided to adapt to fit with the colours of my site. I used a professional designer to create a new logo that incorporated our distinctive baby illustration. I gave her a brief regarding the colours and the kind of feeling I wanted the logo to give. I wanted the baby illustration to become a recognisable image relating to my company, so that it gave a feeling of continuity when used across my business stationery and products."

– Jo Fazel (www.bestbabyshower.co.uk)

"I handed my logo design over to a graphic designer friend, although the final colour choice was made after purchasing three items of clothing, tipping them out of the bag when I got home and falling in love with the colour combination of tangerine, raspberry pink and lime!"

– Sharon-Elaine Chapman (www.thebabycakeboutique.co.uk)

Do not be afraid to get out there and find out what emotions, thoughts and opinions are triggered when a potential customer sees your brand. What do they like? What do they dislike? How does it make them feel? Use social media to ask leading questions. Do not be afraid of the answers or to tweak your brand as you feel is needed.

ACTIVITY #3:
TWO-TIER NAPPY CAKE

by Best Baby Shower (**www.bestbabyshower.co.uk**)

You will need

- Plenty of disposable nappies

- 1 round cake board

- 2 different sized spring form cake tins without the bases to help hold the shape (optional)

- Elastic bands

- 2 x blankets, wraps, towels or muslin cloths

- 1 x washcloth, muslin, bib or bodysuit to cover the top of top tier

- Item of your choice to use inside cake as stabiliser (e.g. brush & comb set/toy/rolled up sleepsuit or bodysuit
- Item for topping the 'cake' such as a soft toy
- Paper shreds as 'icing' (optional)
- Glue dots
- Ribbon to finish

Method

Step 1. Start off by laying out all the 'ingredients' you are going to need – it's easier to have everything to hand once you've started making your nappy cake.

Step 2. Grab the brush and comb set (or roll up a baby sleepsuit), wrap one nappy around it and secure with an elastic band. This is going to act as a stabiliser to help hold together the top and bottom tiers. You can use anything as a stabiliser as long as it is tall enough to stand up an inch or two above the height of the bottom tier of nappies.

Step 3. Continue to wrap more nappies around the stabiliser item, with each nappy slightly overlapping the end of the previous one. Continue until you cannot hold all the nappies around it tightly with your hands and then wrap an elastic band around it.

Step 4. Place your cake board down on your work table and then put the largest of your two spring form cake tins on top. You don't have to use a cake tin but it does make it considerably easier to hold the nappies as you build up the layers.

Step 5. Place your stabiliser item with the nappies wrapped around it down in the middle of the cake board. Continue to wrap nappies around in the overlapping fashion until you cannot fit any more nappies in at the edges of the cake tin. (Note: If you are not using a cake tin then keep wrapping nappies until the tier of nappies is approximately the same size as the cake board underneath. You may need to wrap an elastic band around the nappies and then tuck each extra nappy underneath the elastic band as you go around building up the layers to hold it all together.)

Step 6. Once you have completed your bottom tier, wrap another elastic band around the whole tier and then open the spring form cake tin (if using) and slide it off.

Step 7. Now it's time to wrap the bottom tier. You can use whatever you like provided it's long enough to completely encircle the tier of nappies with enough material to overlap. I find that towels and blankets work well on the bottom tier and that lighter wraps and muslin cloths work well on small tiers. In this example I have used a hooded baby towel. Fold the towel or blanket over and over along its longest length until the width is just slightly wider than the height of the bottom tier of nappies. With a hooded towel it looks best to have the hood part standing up at the front. Lay it out flat on your work table and then pick up the bottom tier and lay it on its end in the middle of the fabric and then fold up one side of the fabric around it and then fold up the other side. I like to tuck one end in between the layers of the other end so that it looks neat and then often is tight enough not to need anything else holding it around the tier. However if this is too fiddly you can just overlap the fabric and hold in place with an elastic band which you will cover with ribbon later on.

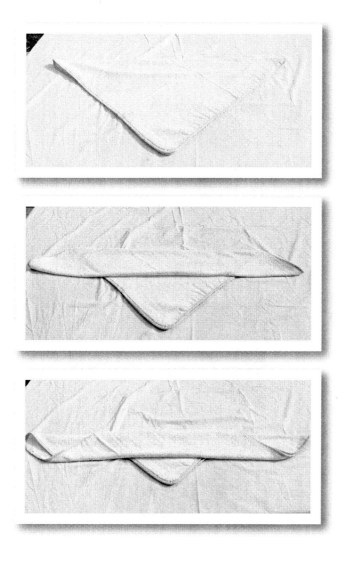

Step 8. Now you can start to build your top tier. Place the smaller of the cake tins on the top of the bottom tier. Wrap a nappy around the stabiliser item that is sticking up through the middle of the

bottom tier. Secure with an elastic band. Continue to wrap nappies around as you did for the bottom tier until the cake tin is full. The tier should be slightly smaller in diameter than the bottom tier. Secure with an elastic band around the whole tier.

Step 9. Now slide off the cake tin and take the washcloth (or bib/other small item of baby clothing) and drape it over the top of the top tier. Secure around the edge with an elastic band. (It will now look a bit like the traditional top of a jam jar.)

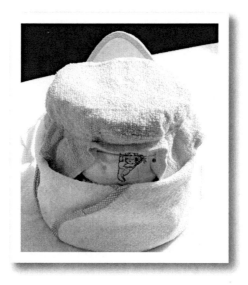

Step 10. Slide the whole top tier off the bottom tier ready to wrap with your muslin cloth/wrap/blanket. Fold the muslin cloth along its length again so that it is just slightly wider than the height of the tier of nappies. Then place your tier on its end in the middle and wrap the muslin cloth around the sides of the tier, covering up the ends of the washcloth which are hanging down the sides of the tier. Secure with an elastic band.

Step 11. Now place the top tier back on top of the bottom tier by sliding it over the stabilising item again and lining up the backs of the top and bottom tier where the material overlaps.

Step 12. If you want to embellish the 'cake' with 'icing' you can use some shredded coloured paper to tuck in around the edge of the top tier between the washcloth on top and the muslin cloth wrapped around the edge.

Step 13. Now you can dress your 'cake' with ribbons of your choice. I like to use a wider plain florist's ribbon with a prettier smaller patterned ribbon (such as the polka-dot ribbon in the picture) over the top. Secure the ends of the florist ribbon together with a glue dot. Cut off enough patterned ribbon to encircle the tier with enough left to tie a bow at the front. Trim any excess ribbon to neaten the finish. Finish by placing your soft toy on the top (you could use a little double-sided sticky tape to hold in place if you wish).

Tips

- To really give your nappy cake the wow factor you can wrap the entire cake in cellophane and finish with a pull bow and lots of colour co-ordinating curling ribbon.

- Don't forget you can design your cake any way you like – use a blanket instead of a towel, build more tiers, hide extra items inside the tiers, work to a particular theme, decorate with flowers or even rolled up sock 'roses' – the choice is yours!

CHAPTER
FOUR
WHERE TO SELL

MARKET RESEARCH

Before setting up a website or making enough products to sink a small ship, you need to do your market research. It is vital to perform an early 'test the market' exercise. Book a small stall at a local market, school fête or even a toddler group; anywhere that you can display your products and engage with potential customers. This does not need to be costly. Always try to haggle the price for your pitch.

You *need* to gather feedback, so take this opportunity to find out:

- what sells well
- what does not sell at all
- what potential customers like
- what potential customers dislike
- what they think of the pricing
- what they think of your brand image
- what they think of your packaging.

Have a list of questions to ask or prepare feedback forms. All you need is a quick list with boxes for marking products, packaging, pricing, etc., out of ten and a space for any comments. The best businesses grow organically and you probably won't get everything right first time so listen to your customers and adapt accordingly.

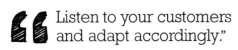 Listen to your customers and adapt accordingly."

Market research does need to be conducted on strangers and not those who know you or have a vested interest in you or your business. Nadine Thomas (**www.nellie-dean.com**) also suggests that it is useful to:

> "start by making items, giving them away and asking for feedback, thereby perfecting your products before launching them to market."

Again, if you are going to do this avoid your friends and family. If your testing leaves you with even more questions then ask other, more established crafting businesses, go to a 'stitch and bitch club' or use craft forums; there is a wealth of knowledge and help out there.

Market research enables you to:

- Gauge interest in your products
- Generate money – which in the early stages you may need to invest in areas such as advertising, marketing, equipment and supplies.
- Iron out any kinks, as hopefully it shall help with any unanswered questions.

HOW I STARTED

I bought £56.65 of wooden party bag fillers from a shopkeeping friend and sold them at school fêtes and village carnivals. 'Daddy Moo' and Charlie would come along and help me set up and then come back to help me pack up.

This enabled me to:

- gauge interest in the fillers

- raise the money I needed to drive Charlie Moo's forward

- talk to potential customers and help perfect my stock choices, pricing and display.

I was actually selling products at a carnival two weeks before Megan's due date! But all the information I was able to collate was vital in developing my stock list, brand and website.

"The market research I carried out was basic. About three months before the business officially started I took a stand at a local craft fair displaying potential products at a variety of different prices. I found that we sold more of the cheaper products. People liked the variety of prices and were complimentary about the more expensive ones but didn't buy them. So I now sell a different range at craft fairs to the one I have online. My online range caters for the premium market, whilst the craft fairs tends to be samples and old stock."

– Caroline Watts (www.carolinewattsembroidery.co.uk)

"Most of my research was done on the internet. Trawling through for hours looking at other websites (lots in the US where I know baby showers are much bigger) to find out what kind of things were being sold. Then looking at parenting forums and also questions being asked on Yahoo! Answers to see what people were looking for or having trouble finding. I now use places like my Facebook Page to put forward potential ideas and get feedback. And of course I spent time discussing plans and potential products with friends and family – mostly those in my target market (women of childbearing age). Not forgetting that I am also my own target market, so I spent a lot of time thinking about products and website visuals – what would I want to buy or have information about?"

– Jo Fazel (www.bestbabyshower.co.uk)

SELLING

The real beauty in making handmade products is the vast amount of places you can sell them, enabling you to tailor your business to your lifestyle. For example, if you are a parent or if you are still in full-time employment (the so-called 5 to 9ers) you can fund the start-up and develop your business in your spare time. Some crafters, especially if what they make is very time-consuming, simply do not have the time to venture to markets to sell in person. Some crafters will relish in the joy of direct selling whereby customers can touch, smell, taste, and be as tactile as they wish to be with their products.

Jamie Fry (**www.creativestores.co.uk/UncleBundleCrafts**) agrees: *"It gives me a buzz and I love the interaction and the direct selling."* In person you can develop relationships and repeat business with your customers, but in comparison, websites produce a sense of anonymity and lack of personal interaction. There are numerous online craft-selling sites such as Etsy and MISI, and gallery-style sites such as UnikGifts and WOWThankYou, which offer a cheap way to reach a large number of potential customers through a readymade audience. However, in my opinion, having your own website for online selling allows you to develop more of an independent brand. The biggest pro is that your virtual shop is open 24 hours a day, meaning even if you are asleep, eating dinner or sitting on a bus, theoretically your site is making *you* money. Now that cannot be bad!

ONLINE CRAFT SITES

"Sites such as Etsy and Folksy are a great way to start a business. As with any online business though you should be driving your own sales by doing marketing and PR. Depending on your product some people may buy after discovering you by chance, but to build a sustainable business you need to draw buyers in yourself."

– Noisette Marketing (www.noisettemarketing.com)

You cannot just set up a website or onlineshop and expect orders to come flying in. If only it was that easy! It takes time, good PR, marketing, excellent customer service and testimonials to develop a customer base and get your name out there. The first year is usually the hardest, so do not get despondent if the results of all your hard work are not instantaneous.

Below is an overview of each of the major craft-selling websites, and a few others I discovered along the way. All prices/fees/commissions were correct at the time of writing.

Etsy (www.etsy.com)

"Etsy is all about reconnecting producer and consumer. We aim to highlight the true value of handmade goods and to encourage awareness of the social and environmental implications of production and consumption."

– Etsy UK (www.facebook.com/EtsyUK)

Etsy is the world's largest online handcraft marketplace. You are charged a fee to list your products and a 3.5% fee once that product sells. All fees are paid on a monthly basis through PayPal or by credit card. You can easily integrate an Etsy shop into your website/Facebook page, giving you a simple and easy way to drive traffic from your site straight to your shop. There is an extensive list of FAQs which I suggest you read before signing up.

As Etsy is worldwide, their databases are huge, which is great in terms of potential customers but means it can be difficult to get noticed as a seller. You will need to make your listings look as professional as possible and make really good use of keywords (the words customers type into a search engine to find a product). It is also important to share your unique Etsy URL (**www.etsy.com/shop/PoppySparkles**, for example) and promote yourself. Etsy have a host of materials to help you, including an email bulletin for sellers about marketing your shop and promoting yourself online. Crafters I have spoken to suggested that networking with other Etsy sellers is also beneficial for promoting your shop. Etsy's Teams (**www.etsy.com/teams**) are a good place to network. There's a Team (essentially an online community) for everything from UK or European Sellers, to nichier ones based on your specific craft, or for people who share a common factor such as being a mum or an army wife.

Although Etsy is based in America it is becoming better known in the UK and there is a drive from Etsy to actively promote the site through PR and events.

Folksy (www.folksy.com)

Folksy charges 20p to list a product and a 5% commission once the product sells. Fees are paid monthly via PayPal and are now VATable. As with Etsy, you can also use an application to display your shop on your Facebook page; though Folksy is restricted to UK-based sellers.

Folksy recently changed their criteria and a number of products are no longer considered to be handmade, instead they are 'assembled'. For example, charms that are readily available, especially if they are threaded on a chain, and candles in china teacups, although the candles are melted and their cups handpicked. Ensure that you spend time reading through their support pages and that your products do qualify for the site.

"[With] Folksy, you do have to continually upload but you can also 'join in' with the marketing, e.g. I wrote a Folksy Friday blog for the site profiling my favourite shops, and that was on the front page for a week. You can also join their forum and chat to other crafters. I feel it's a lot more pro-active and friendly than Etsy. Plus their support staff are very efficient; I emailed them a query and had a response the same evening. You do have to keep on top to stay on top, but there doesn't seem to be the same fight for the top spot."

– Dufflebobble Crafts
(www.folksy.com/shops/DufflebobbleCrafts)

MISI – Make It Sell It (www.misi.co.uk)

UK-based MISI aims to help buyers find quality handmade products with a personal touch. Launched in October 2008, MISI won Highly Commended in Best Start Up at the MumprenuerUK Awards 2009. The site has 3,000 sellers and reaches 75,000 visitors per month.

MISI boasts a free for life shop, free blog for sellers, free domain (i.e. **yourshop.misi.co.uk**), low commission of 3% on sales and 20p per listing regardless of the quantity. MISI really does seem like a great starting point.

Other sites

WowThankYou (www.wowthankyou.co.uk)

After failing to find affordable UK handmade gifts online, Tracey Kifford decided that she wanted to replicate her love of craft fairs online, with a modern, contemporary feel. WowThankYou's website design, functionality and concept is based on the feedback of over 400 UK crafters – in effect they designed *their* perfect online selling platform.

"The sellers are the driving force behind all website development – everything is discussed with them before being implemented (or not) – this is their website to mould as they want."

– Tracey Kifford (www.wowthankyou.co.uk)

A sellers panel reviews and approves or declines new crafters. WowThankYou is looking for products that are:

- handmade in the UK (by the seller)
- unique – not already on sale through the site
- well photographed
- competitively priced
- complementary to the items already listed.

WowThankYou's other USP is that they plough all their marketing and advertising efforts into campaigns targeted at non-crafters'. There is a *one-off* joining fee, which is £30, and this money is put straight back into their effective marketing approach. Commission is 10% of the sales price, excluding the P&P but there are no other fees or charges. They do, however, ask sellers to stay with them for 12 months and to practice price parity on any rival sites – which, as we discussed before, is good practice anyway.

UnikGifts (www.UnikGifts.co.uk)

UnikGifts is the brainchild of Anna Matthews and Sarah Davies. Keen crafters themselves, they decided to set up a gallery-style site to showcase the huge number of very talented people that were not represented online. There are no listing fees and commission is negotiated with each maker (between 15% and 50%). Unlike other sites UnikGifts play an active role in the experience a customer will have:

> "We send out the products; everything comes into us for quality review and to be personally wrapped. We feel it is important that we control everything. This way, if we are not satisfied with the end result for some reason, we can control the process."
>
> **– Sarah Davies**

Crafters have to fit within the UnikGifts ethos of unique, handmade, high quality and preferably made of natural materials.

YOUR OWN WEBSITE

There are many free or low-cost options when it comes to building your own website, even one with its own shop. You do not even need to be a computer wiz. I use Create (**www.create.net**). It's easy to use, fees are low and the support network is second to none; they are always on hand to help. Building your own website allows you to design pages and a layout that reflects you, your products and your brand – something you can't always do with a third party selling site – but on the flipside you will need to think about running costs, monthly subscription fees and merchant charges.

Here are my key points to think about when developing a website:

- You will need to buy and register your domain name (URL). Do you want to have a .co.uk or a .com? Are both available? Search on sites like 123reg (**www.123reg.com**) or Namesco (**www.names.co.uk**) to see if your company name is available. A co.uk is normally around £6 for two years.

- There are plenty of user-friendly platforms available, enabling you to easily create and edit your site. Check out: **Create.net**, **WordPress.org** (you can add shopping functionality), **Zen-cart.com** for an online shop, **Webs.com** and **Moonfruit.com**. These types of platforms have ready-made templates which as your web skills develop you will easily be able to tweak as required.

- You need an eye-catching home page that is free of clutter but also makes it clear exactly what you do.

- Ensure your site is easy to navigate and logically structured. Always get friends and family to test its usability before making anything live.

- We cannot buy what we cannot see so ensure your images are clear and look professional (see Chapter Five for more on this).

- Look at your competitors' sites. What do you like about them? What don't you like? Make a list and work through these points on your own website.

- Use the same colours on and offline to keep your branding consistent.

- Target your content to your intended audience and make it clear what you want your visitors to do next, i.e. buy from you, contact you, visit you at an event, etc.

- Keep your content relevant but don't try to overuse keywords in an attempt to please search engines. This can actually get your site blacklisted. Also, try to keep the content fresh so that search engines have new things to find.

- Make it easy for customers to purchase your products, e.g. ensure there aren't too many clicks between them adding items to the basket and checking out. Analyse your site as if you were a customer and also review other sites' shopping facilities.

- Build links with other credible websites (known as Google Juice). The more links you have with other sites (especially those of high ranking) the higher your Google ranking should be. Have a dedicated page on your website and swap reciprocal links with ten sites to start off with. Ideally you want to link with websites that have a Google ranking of three and over (check on **www.prchecker.info**) and that are relevant to your business. For example, my site links to baby, children and party suppliers and local Dorset businesses.

- Ask for advice on forums and discussion boards. There is a wealth of free knowledge and advice amongst small business owners and there's usually someone who's experienced a similar problem and is happy to help.

I started researching websites just before Megan was born. At first I used Webs (**www.webs.com**) as it is free. Once I got an idea of what all the symbols were and how to do basic things like editing a page and adding links I felt that the look and feel of the templates available were quite limiting and I failed to get the end result I was really after. In time I felt confident enough to work with something a bit more challenging, so I decided to try Create (**www.create.net**) as it had a free 30-day trial. By the time my trial came to an end I had built a site I was happy with. Charlie Moo's current look has developed over time – as my skills have developed I've been able to change the look and feel – but the great thing about the Create platform is the abundance of excellent templates for complete novices.

"I chose my website because the hosting company was run by a friend of my husband so I could ask for any help I needed. Once the template was up and running, I was able to create and edit posts with ease. I use osCommerce (**www.oscommerce.com**) on my site and though I don't have a web design background I am lucky enough to have a very technical husband who helps me when I get stuck. Apart from advertising I do not really spend a lot of time on my website as it is so easy for my customers to use. Writing the descriptions is what takes up my time. I tend to do all my website work in the evening when I am usually too tired or have finished my sewing. I have had my website for 18 months and haven't looked back. I used to list on Folksy but found that I wasn't selling anything so decided to sell direct instead. I also find that I have much more flexibility with my own website than I had with Folksy. Financially I am also better off as my website costs me £50 per year for unlimited bandwidth and web-space, but with Folksy it was 20p per item plus 5% commission, which is quite expensive when you have well over 200 products."

– Sarah Smith (www.silverbirchcrafts.co.uk)

Viv from Poppy Sparkles (**www.poppysparkles.co.uk**) echoes my opinion on developing your own website:

"I'm very conscious of my image but with two young children, creating my own website that had the image I wanted was too much when I first started. Once I was able to take that step I found that my own website generated more sales than Folksy or Etsy and I'm really glad I did it. In some ways I wish I'd done it sooner, but getting a website when I did was right for me as I'd worked out what I was doing in terms of my style, etc. I'd been faffing with trying to create a shop using WordPress – my hubby is a fan, but it was too hard for me and really did drain my time– when I discovered Create (**www.create.net**)! I've since discovered that there are a number of easy solutions for creating a website for people like me whose skills only stretch so far! And as my skills and confidence improved I've given my website a new look to make sure it is the best it can be. I'd love to have the funds to pay a pro to do it, but that's beyond my reach at the moment."

USEFUL INFORMATION FOR SELLING ONLINE

If you're still feeling confused then read through all the information for each site – especially their FAQ – and get the opinions of other crafters and make a list of pros and cons for each, including the prices you can charge, fees, commissions and margin.

> **Remember price**
>
> Go back to your pricing formula and add in all the fees (listing fees, admin fees, PayPal/merchant fees, etc.) you will incur on third party sites. Remember, these will eat into your profit.

Do not spread yourself too thinly or you may struggle to keep up with your orders. Start with one or two sites and see how you get on. If one isn't working for you and you have low sales, shut it down and move to another site.

If you decide not to sell online at all, it is still worthwhile having some kind of online presence, whether that be a Facebook page or a brief website which has contact and ordering information, details of events you will be attending, testimonials and product images.

CRAFT FAIRS AND MARKETS

Traditional markets are a great place to meet a variety of customers. The early bird catches the worm – you can be making money from 6am whereas most conventional shops do not open till 9am. Markets attract a different type of customer, drawn in by the hustle and bustle, hunting for a bargain. This type of fast-paced selling invokes a sense of urgency and more impulse buys than the calm and tranquillity of a shop; plus there is usually a much larger footfall. However, if you do not fancy a large, outdoor, traditional market there is a variety of market situations, school fêtes, craft fairs, and carnivals to suit your needs.

Build confidence

If you are shy or timid then consider using online selling until you have built up the confidence in yourself and your products to sell face-to-face.

The following skills will be hugely beneficial to succeeding at a market:

● Passion – if you are happy, approachable and passionate and know your products inside out then this will put your potential customers at ease and draw them in.

● Being personable – smile, engage and be positive.

● Being a morning person – you will need the ability to rise early, work long hours and still be cheery and approachable.

● Good communication skills – you will spend a huge proportion of your day talking to people.

● Understand the competition – research who sells at the market, what they are selling, and at what price.

- Be knowledgeable and persuasive – in order to sell, it is best to stick to proven sales techniques. KNOW the features of your product and what benefit it would bring to your customer, be certain of why your customer NEEDS your product, how it is relevant to them now and why they must buy it.

Insurance

When selling or exhibiting, ensure that you have the correct insurances in place.

Public liability insurance covers any awards of damages given to a member of the public because of an injury or damage to their property caused by you or your business. It also covers any related:

- legal fees

- costs

- expenses

- hospital treatment, including ambulance costs, that the NHS may claim from you

Source: Business Link (**www.businesslink.gov.uk**)

Product liability insurance covers you in the event that you are held liable for damage or injury arising from defects in your product, design or manufacture. Your products must be 'fit for purpose' and if a product you have manufactured or supplied (whether for free or sold) is deemed faulty or causes damage or injury to someone, then you may be subject to a claim against you for compensation.

Equipment

You will need:

- A gazebo or market stall, including covers and slips if you are at an outside event (these can usually be hired from the council)

- Table(s) – look for strong sturdy tables that fold down for transporting and that you can carry and set up by yourself

- Tablecloths

- Display stands

- Price lists

- Business cards or flyers

- Carrier/paper bags

- Cash tin or money belt

- Appropriate clothing for all weather conditions

- Refreshments – it's more cost-effective to bring your own, and hopefully you'll be too busy to go and buy anything!

- Consider having a demonstration area, depending on your craft, if there's room, and if you have someone who can help run the stall.

Research

When deciding whether to book an event, do your research. Here are some hints and tips, questions to ask the organisers and the best ways to make event selling work for you.

- Find out what **other businesses are exhibiting** and the other products that will be for sale; the organiser will be able to give you a list or it may be on their website. It's important to determine whether it is pure crafts or will also include sellers with mass-produced goods. This could affect your sales as your products may look expensive in comparison.

- **Site location** – is it in a well populated area? What was the footfall for previous events? Is there adequate parking for visitors? If you have the chance, pay a visit beforehand and see for yourself. Pretend you are a potential customer; would you travel to this location?

- **Your location** – where exactly in the room will you be positioned? Are a table and chair (and anything else such as power points and refreshments) provided?

- **Size of the room** – is it a good size? Have most of the pitches been sold? A half empty room can make you look lost, and potential customers will be put off.

- **Advertising** – how many leaflets are being distributed and where (targeted or random)? Will it be advertised in the local newspapers and on local radio? Are there posters near the venue and surrounding area? Will there be signs on the day? Will it be listed online?

- **Tailor your stock** to the audience the event is marketed at.

"At a school fête I take lots of pocket money items, personalised kids stuff, etc. whereas at a ladies pamper evening I place the emphasis on ladies products or items for the home."

– Nadine Thomas (www.nellie-dean.com)

Make sure you **know your rights** as well as those of the consumer. Unlike distance selling, customers do not have the right to a cooling-off period, so if they change their mind you are not obliged to refund them. However, if your item is faulty or not as described then think about your reputation and please give the money back. Think how you would feel if you were the customer.

If you cannot find the type of event you're looking for in your area then why not organise one yourself?

Sales

No two events will be the same. At the end of each one, make sure you take clear and useful notes about what worked – and what didn't – in terms of your products, your display and the event itself. Try not to go with huge expectations but make a clear goal about what you want to achieve.

"I have found that you cannot predict how a fair or event will go. The ones where you think you'll do a roaring trade, you find yourself doubting your business and wondering why you haven't done as well as you'd hoped. Then there's the small event where you do really well and equally wonder why. Like the one I did last year: a winter's evening too close to Christmas for comfort, icy roads, hardly advertised, small room, hardly any tables, but everyone that came in seemed to buy something. That's the kind of event I like!"

– Nadine Thomas (www.nellie-dean.com)

"You need a lot of stock that has a low purchase price (£2-3), which is another reason I increased my product base from just cards. I find that paying £25 a pitch at a craft fair is not worthwhile; whilst it gives me a buzz and I love the interaction and the direct selling, I sometimes only just make my money back."

– Jamie Fry (www.creativestores.co.uk/UncleBundleCrafts)

Most of my products have a 50% mark-up, which means if I was to pay £25 for a pitch I would need £50 worth of sales to break even (excluding my time, petrol and any advertising materials I purchased for the event). This is important to take into consideration especially if, like Jamie, your products have a low retail value – he would need to sell 50-100 items. This may be easy, it may not, so make sure you have a range of products. For example, it is good to have a couple of Guide your customers and help make it an easy decision to buy." expensive items (£20+), some medium items (£10+) and lots of things under £5, as these appeal to children and are good gifts, stocking fillers, etc. Advertise them as such too – guide your customers wherever you can and help make it an easy decision to buy.

If you can, take projects you are working on with you as customers will enjoy seeing you create your products. It also enhances your story and the visual appeal of your products. I believe that if potential customers can see products mid-creation and understand the work that goes into them, they have a greater respect for the process and are thus more prepared to pay a premium for handmade.

SELLING WHOLESALE

This simply means selling your goods to retailers who then sell to the end customer (as opposed to you selling directly). Generally you make a smaller profit per item because the reseller also needs to make their margin, but wholesaling usually involves larger quantities so you get increased volume. It is a win-win situation; your products are out on the shelves and the retailer increases their range of unique handmade products – something severely lacking on the high street.

Why is wholesale useful? It increases your potential market and customer base, and it frees you up for creating rather than selling your products.

When selling direct to customers you are using your retail price (see page 19). However, for wholesalers you need to use your trade price. If you have a recommend retail price, or RRP, then look to offer wholesalers a 50% discount on that (as long as you still make a reasonable profit). It's good to have an RRP to keep pricing parity across your various selling channels.

> "If you are supplying to local shops and selling locally yourself (at fairs, etc.) you have to be wary of not undercutting the shops."
>
> **– Nadine Thomas (www.nellie-dean.com)**

You also do not want too many businesses in the same area selling your products as it dilutes their uniqueness.

Do's and Don'ts

● DO have low minimum order quantities.

● DO have a postage charge for smaller orders and then free carriage for larger ones, (e.g. I charge £3.95 for P&P on orders under £100 and free P&P for orders over £100).

● DO insist on payment upfront for the initial order (use a proforma – an invoice that needs to be paid prior to products being dispatched). For subsequent orders offer a 30-day credit invoice, but keep an eye on the amount of credit you are offering to each retailer.

● DON'T be afraid to say NO, especially in the beginning when you're trying to market a new product. If their business doesn't suit your style, your ethos or your pricing structure then turn it down.

● DO have a trade enquiry form on your website.

● DO optimise your website for wholesale, as well as your industry/product, by including keywords such as wholesale, stockists and trade. Make sure you have a page on your site dedicated to trade accounts.

● DO subscribe to relevant trade magazines. Sending press releases to them can be a good way to get your products in front of wholesale buyers.

"Consider paying to register on wholesale directories. When I started out I paid to be listed on TheWholesaler because it appeared highly on search engines. In time my website started to rank highly for wholesale searches too. On the plus side I did get wholesale orders through it, on the down side it's not cheap!"

– Elizabeth Geldart (www.chiggs.co.uk)

SALE OR RETURN

Sale or return is a really good way to get your products into shops. Basically, a shop will hold your stock for a designated period of time and pay you for any that they sell. Those items that do not sell are returned to you. It is a perfect (and inexpensive) way for retailers to test the market. If your products sell well, then ask the retailer to start purchasing them as wholesale instead. This means you have a more regular income and avoid having unpaid-for stock in various retail outlets.

You have to consider a few things, including the fact that retailers will add 100%+ to the item's price, especially if you take into consideration where it will sell. For example, shops in London will charge a higher premium than anywhere else in the country. The general industry rule is that the retailer will multiply your trade price by 2.3, so ensure you take this into consideration when setting your trade prices and RRPs.

For sale or return the shop will have a general rule for their commission or cut, which tends to be lower than when buying the products outright.

There are many pros and cons to consider with sale or return and you have to be on the ball! Regularly check your sums, and the shops' stock, to ensure that this is a worthwhile exercise and a good direction for your business to continue in.

Hints and Tips

● Think about what makes you unique. What is your USP? Do you offer something that nobody else does? What makes you stand out from the crowd? Retail outlets will love this; everyone likes to think they lead a trend.

- Decide beforehand whether your products have an RRP, in which case you might get less once the shop takes their commission (which can be anything from 25% to 50%).

- Know your product and prices inside out. Start pricing high; you can always bring prices down but it is very hard to go the other way. Plus it leaves room to negotiate.

- Make sure you and the retailer have records of all the items they have in stock, as well as any returned to you. It is very important to keep track of this. You think you'll remember everything later on but you won't!

- Offer point of sale (POS). This is a very useful tool to help the customer relate to you, your product and your story. Browse your target shops and see how your merchandising could fit into their layout.

  Find out if the retail outlet wants you to be responsible for the display of your products (this is common in the USA, but less so in the UK). If they do, consider how you might like the display to look and label your belongings if you want them back. If you are not involved in POS then ask a friend to check out how the retail outlet is displaying your products (almost like a secret shopper). This will help you to judge if it is the right outlet for you.

- If the retail outlet is VAT-registered – even if you are not – this will affect the end price, so configure your prices accordingly by quoting everyone the net trade price.

- Don't undersell yourself as people may take advantage or not value your work/product.

- Imagine if you get large orders and have to make 100 items a day and it becomes a chore, or simply unachievable. At what price point does it become worthwhile for to you to employ someone to do it for you?

- Do not give up your profit!

- Agree how long the items will stay in the shop, or how you can help manage the supply to keep it fresh and new.

- Be prepared for returns being damaged and make sure that the outlet takes responsibility for breakages/soiling or you will end up covering the costs.

- Provide branded packaging for your items, for example, supplying jewellery with boxes and/or bags; but do make sure you factor this extra cost into your price. This will also make your brand look more professional, to both the customer and the retailer.

- Include business cards or an informational leaflet inside, add stickers with your details on, use themed packaging, etc. Some retail outlets do not like this, so be discreet or check with them first.

- Judge your stock levels and do not oversell in any one town/village/location. Choose the best fit for your products and start there. If they are not keen, visit your second option, and so on.

- Make sure that you and the retailers know when payment is due to you and jointly agree how payment will be made (bank transfer, cash, cheque, PayPal, credit card, etc.). Bear in mind what your bank or merchant will charge you for each type of transaction.

- If the shop owner says "No thank you", try to get some feedback but don't pester, just thank them and walk away. This makes it easier to go back with another idea in due course. Shops HATE being cornered!

These tips have been put together with the help of Emma Pattullo (**www.platform22.co.uk**).

GALLERIES

Galleries, whether on or offline, work just like any other reseller – either by wholesale or by sale or return. Hawthorn, a craft gallery and haberdashery in Blandford, Dorset, sells work by local and national contemporary craft designers alongside a selection of essential and vintage haberdashery.

And this isn't just happening in Dorset. In a poor economic climate there simply isn't an abundance of jobs available in the creative sector, so instead recent graduates have been developing their own businesses using the galleries. Graduates have time on their hands, and usually fewer overheads, enabling them to develop more 'selfish' businesses.

Galleries offer a perfect forum for you to sell your products and reach a wider audience, but they also provide an outlet that appeals to a certain type of customer, one you might not normally reach. Customers shopping in galleries are generally prepared to pay a higher premium than those shopping at markets.

There are a vast variety of ways in which to sell your handcrafted products both online and offline. Some will be successful for your business, others won't. Do your research, be knowledgeable and be prepared to change and adapt along the way.

ACTIVITY #4:
DRIBBLE BIB

by That's Sew Laura
(**thatssewlaura.co.uk**)

Bandana-style dribble bibs have become increasingly popular over the last couple of years. This particular bib is great at absorbing dribble, as the fleece on the back stops it from soaking through onto clothing. The pattern I designed is short so it sits nicely under the chin but doesn't take over your child's entire outfit! It should take you approximately 20 minutes to make the bib. It's a lovely, easy and practical project!

You will need:

- A piece of 100% cotton fabric for the front
- A piece of fleece for the back
- Either Velcro or poppers for the closure
- Scissors
- Thread

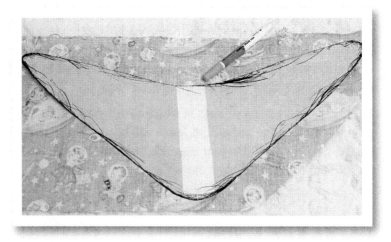

Step 1. Make a template approximately 44cm across by 16cm deep. This bib will fit a child from newborn to approximately two years. Draw around the template on the back of your cotton and fleece, then cut out the shapes.

Step 2. Pin the two pieces together with the pattern facing in.

Step 3. Stitch around the outside, approximately half a centimetre from the edge. Leave a gap of about 4cm so that you can turn it out.

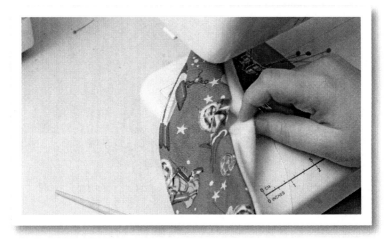

Step 4. Using the gap, pull the bib the right way out. (Tip: You can use a chopstick to make sure everything is pushed out properly.) You should now have a bib . . . with a hole in it! Turn the edges of the hole in on themselves, then close the hole so it's flush with the edge of the bib and then pin it in place. You can then pin around the edge of the bib to get a nice even edge when top stitching.

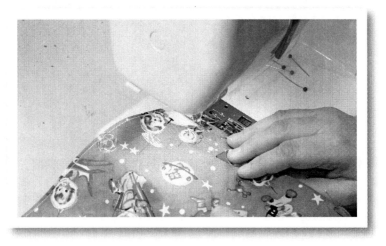

Step 5. Top stitch all the way around the edge of the bib, around 2mm in from the edge. This secures the hole and gives the bib a nice professional finish.

Step 6. Now it's time to add your closure. I use poppers which I add using this handy tool. Alternatively, you can stitch Velcro on to the ends of the bib to close or use stitch-on poppers.

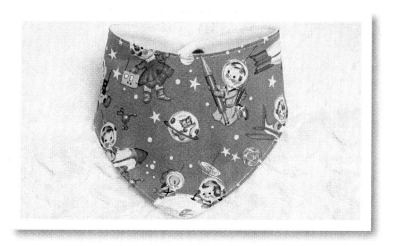

Step 7. And you're done! Now find your dribble monster and try it out!

© 2012 That's Sew Laura. If you wish to use this pattern or tutorial please give full credit.

CHAPTER

 FIVE

VISUAL
MERCHANDISING

ow you display your products is as important as the effort you put into making them. If your table displays are not visually appealing, or your online images are not clear and enticing then you will struggle to make that sale.

 How you display your products is as important as the effort you put into making them."

AT CRAFT FAIRS AND MARKETS

Think about how you will catch the eye of potential customers from a distance. Have a banner handmade or printed – pop-up or vinyl banners can be picked up for less than £40 on eBay and Vistaprint. I wanted the Charlie Moo's banner to reflect my business brand and ethos, so mine was handpainted by a local artist.

Cover your tables with a cloth that matches your branding/colour theme and provides the best backdrop for your items (e.g. black is good for jewellery), or look at having one specially designed for you. I have a few metres of cow-print fabric that I use.

Look to add variety, texture and individuality when displaying your products – shelving, tree bark/branches, baskets, etc. can all be improvised and are inexpensive. Add height to your display whenever possible, as laid-down items are less visually appealing. Shelves are great but if your budget is limited or you can't find the right size, then get some cardboard boxes and either wrap them in paper or drape fabric over them to give the illusion of height.

Place any larger items at the back, smaller ones at the front and group similar ranges together where possible. Display products in groups of three or five (odd numbers balance best) and position your strongest range in the area most visible to browsers. Place your cheaper, more tactile products at the front, as this will encourage interaction from potential customers.

"Try to put the bestselling items at the front, and I was recently advised to have a large statement piece to draw customers to the table."

– Nadine Thomas (www.nellie-dean.com)

Make sure everything is priced as customers don't always like to ask, plus it makes it easier for you. (By law there should be a price list and place of manufacture on display.) You need labels that are clean and clear. A handwritten label on crafted paper for a one-off handmade gift box speaks volumes about the quality of the item. Alternatively, print them off on your computer, get your children to write them (if appropriate) or be creative. Don't forget to clearly highlight any offers such as 'Buy two, get third free'.

If possible, find out before the event exactly where your stall will be situated. You could even request a specific area if you know the venue. Then make sure you maximise your space. Remember to use the front of the table; items can hang down over the edge. It makes great additional space, maximising your selling potential and making your stall look even more appealing. Stand back and view your stall objectively. Have you achieved maximum impact?

Take photos of your stall for your site/social media and Tweet live if you have the time. As mentioned earlier, note down what works, what doesn't, and any customer feedback for future reference.

If you are selling outside in a gazebo, do not expect potential customers to 'walk into' the space. Use tables to dictate the selling space and direct people. Consider where they will approach from – is it from the left, right or the centre? Remember, the back and sides are your windows so display items here. Say hello, smile and be approachable, but don't pounce!

If you don't have business cards (and these days it's so cheap to print a few that it seems a missed opportunity not to) then print out your details (name, logo, website, special offers, etc.) and hand them out to each potential customer. Try to take people's contact details and build up a database of contacts who have shown an interest in your products (you can follow up with an email or mailing). Always have a pad and pen available to capture details, and consider conducting a prize draw by placing a pad and slips next to a box and encouraging people to enter by leaving an email address or business card. We all love a freebie!

These tips have been put together with the help of Deborah Dobson (**www.rightangle.uk.com**) and Cathy Taylor (**www.sweetheartknits.co.uk**).

IMAGES

Never underestimate the power of a carefully created image. I have seen so many beautifully constructed websites using images that are poor, grainy, blurred or even too small, which completely ruins the overall appeal. Bad images do not invite people to buy from you; they may even think you're hiding something, or simply don't care enough to supply good photographs. Inviting, detailed product images are essential because customers are unable to physically engage with your items. You don't need a flash, expensive camera, nor do you need to be an excellent photographer. I would suggest, though, that you do invest some money in a tripod in order to eliminate shaky images. Again, it doesn't have to be the best one on the market, but do look for one that can rotate the camera down, so you can take images from above.

Image styles

There are two main styles that are used – lifestyle and still life on white – and both have their own merits. It really does depend on what you are planning to do with the images so do give this some consideration.

Lifestyle

Lifestyle photography shows your product in a particular setting, or being used. You can really go to town with these types of image. Examples would be children wearing the clothing, jewellery being worn, a cup being drunk from, or even staging a scene. Imagine a party – a dressed table, an array of gorgeous handmade fabric party bags(!), a tier of decorated cupcakes in match-ing cake cases, pitchers of juice and bunting – all designed to  make potential customers want to recreate the atmosphere and the feelings that this scene provokes. Scene-setting can encourage potential customers to buy more items in order to recreate the bigger picture. It also draws their attention to items they may not have looked at individually.

This type of image is also useful to show scale. As a customer there is nothing worse than an item arriving and realising that it is smaller or larger than you anticipated.

Still Life on White

Still life on white photography is as it sounds – your product is photographed against a pure white, crisp background. This style is very popular for individual product pages, as there aren't any distractions – the product is all you see. Take the photograph against the most uniform, whitest backdrop you can, be it a sheet, wall or just paper. You could also consider using a light box – buy one or make your own using white paper.

You may find that even though you have photographed your product on a white background, the result may not look pure white. If it is a pinkish shade it will be too warm and natural light or tungsten light may have been used. If it is a greyish or blue colour the image is too cold. To counteract this, ensure that your product is a reasonable distance away from your background and then flood this space with light. It is best to do this in a light tent or on paper. Ensure that the light is fairly even all around. A fairly reasonable shot can be taken with the simplest of desk lamps. Do not be afraid to use editing software in order to 'create' white or to crop/cut the image and place it on a white background. Don't worry too much if it is not pure white; as long as it is a solid colour, magazines will still be able to use it by cropping the product out. The most important thing to remember is that the product should be lit well and evenly so – aim more for this than for the white background.

Magazine editors will normally request still life on white images as they can easily be cut to suit the layout of the magazine. If you are lucky enough to be approached by a magazine and are taking your own images, do not be afraid to ask them exactly what they require – it is worth going that extra mile and sending them bespoke images.

Still Life

If the images are for your website then do not be afraid to use a coloured background, but keep to one colour and make sure the fabric or paper used does not detract from the product. You could even use material, such as velvet which works well as it absorbs the light giving a more even tone.

Shoot your images in both landscape and portrait as then you have both options readily available.

Size really does matter

The next thing you need to consider is the size of the images – by which I mean resolution, not dimensions. Magazines will require the image to be in high resolution for print purposes (300 dots per inch or dpi is the minimum) and they usually prefer square. Bear in mind that a standard image is oblong, so consider this when framing your shot as you may have to adjust and/or edit the image later.

Website images are normally 72dpi as that is screen resolution so anything above that is wasted (and can make for slow page loading). Most image software packages give you the option to generate a low resolution version. It's worth doing this as you can also use them in press releases, resulting in a smaller file size which is more sociable for emailing and downloading from the site.

Lights, Camera, Action!

Light plays a huge role in how your images will look. Natural light is always better but you will need to consider harsh light and shadows. If you are shooting indoors then try to avoid flash, as this can be harsh and cause dramatic shadows. Ideally, shoot in daylight and use additional lighting, looking out for shadows and moving items as appropriate. Avoid using tungsten lights (normal household lightbulbs) as this can cause your images to have a yellow tinge.

As an example, the below images were taken with a normal point and shoot compact camera. The first was taken in the evening with the lights on and using the camera's flash. Can you see the harsh shadows and shades it has produced? The second was taken in the evening under ordinary house lights. Can you see the dullness and poor quality due to insufficient light? The third image was taken in daylight next to a window and is clearly the best of the three. These images are just a guide to demonstrate my point about the use of lighting.

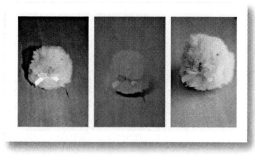

Don't be afraid to try different lighting, styles and scene-setting with your images. Just as you have been creative with your products, be the same with your images. Every image speaks a thousand words and every image represents your product, your brand, your business and YOU.

This photography section has been written with help from product photographers Anna Brim (**www.alohaphotography.co.uk**) and Louise Jolley (**www.louisejolleyphotography.com**).

Visual merchandising is all about presenting your products in order to highlight their features and benefits. The overall purpose being to attract, engage and motivate the customer towards making that magical purchase.

Ensure that your displays and online images:

- make it easier for your customer to locate desired categories and merchandise

- make it easier for the customer to self-select

- make it possible for the shopper to co-ordinate and accessorise, e.g. show bags and jewellery of the same colour or theme together, or set the scene using your products

- recommend, highlight and demonstrate particular products

- inform the customer about the product in an effective and creative way

- make proper arrangements in such a way that increase sales.

ACTIVITY #5:
APRON

by Laura Clempson (www.cupcakesforclara.com)

A children's apron to protect their clothes when baking, painting and waving their mucky fingers around!

You will need:

- Hard-wearing cotton fabric

- Strong cotton tape

- Cotton that matches fabric

- Bias binding

- Pins

- Fabric marker

- Sewing machine

- Scissors

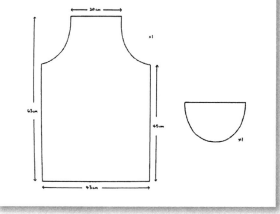

Step 1. Copy, enlarge and cut out the pattern pieces.

Step 2. Fold the cotton fabric in half lengthwise, and using a fabric marker trace around half of the pattern, placing the centre of the apron pattern on the fabric fold. Allow a 3cm seam allowance and cut out.

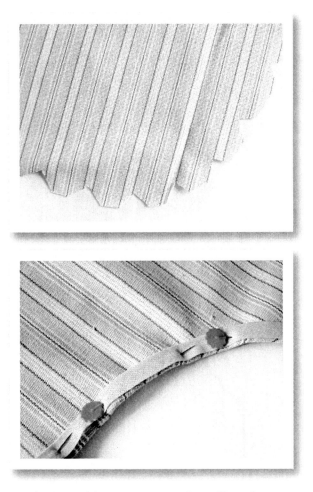

Step 3. Unfold the fabric. Cut several small V shapes into the curved edges. Fold the seam over to the rear and cover the seam edge with bias binding, as shown in the picture, to create a tidy edge. Pin, and carefully machine sew.

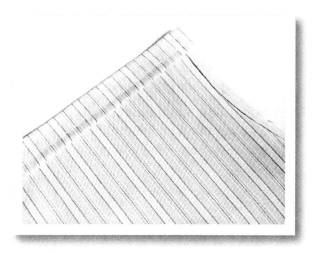

Step 4. Double fold the apron side seams under. Pin and machine sew. Do the same with the top and bottom seams.

Step 5. Cut three lengths of cotton tape: two 55cm long and one 50cm long. Double turn under the ends of the two longer lengths, and sew a strong square shape as shown in the picture. Fold under the other end of each tape and machine sew to the back of the

apron sides, just below the curved edges, with the same strong square shape.

Step 6. Stitching the same shape, attach the final length of cotton tape to the top of the apron. This is the neck strap.

Step 7. To add the pocket turn the seam under on the pocket piece, cutting small V shapes in the curves as before, and carefully sew. Pin it to the apron in the desired position and sew on (twice to add strength).

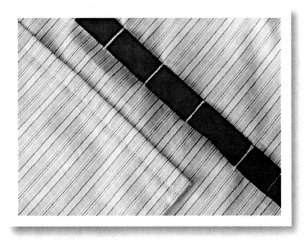

Step 8. To add a utility belt cut a length of cotton tape 10cm longer than the width of the apron. Turn under the ends and pin across the apron, with the ends attaching at the back. Sew vertical lines across the tape, as shown in the picture.

Step 9. The apron can easily be embellished with an embroidered picture, wording or a patch of contrasting fabric.

© Laura Clempson, cupcakesforclara@yahoo.co.uk

CHAPTER

SIX

MARKETING

nce you have developed the fundamentals of your business, including:

- making the products
- devising your pricing formulas
- branding yourself and products
- deciding where and how you will sell
- organising your visual merchandising

the next step is marketing. I know it might sound daunting, but you don't need a marketing degree or years of experience. What you do need is a passion for your products and a commonsense plan. Obviously you want to keep the costs down, and the best way to do that is to do it yourself. There are lots of free marketing channels, so lets look at the biggest opportunities.

PR

I do all my own PR and have been very successful over the years, from small mentions in my local paper to fullpage spreads in national magazines such as *Prima* and *Craftseller*. Obviously writing your own press releases will save you money; you know your range and your business better than anyone and it's good practice. Plus it enables you to personally build relationships with journalists. I started off by collecting email addresses of local newspapers, magazines and radio stations. Check out the editor page – it's all detailed there – and you can usually find most of this information online too.

Journalists are sent so many press releases that they don't have time to download and carefully read every single attachment. So, forget the niceties. The most affective way to send a press release is as the body of the email and to get straight to the point. Attach a Word/PDF version and any relevant images (at an email-friendly size).

How to layout a press release

LOGO/BANNER

Press Release

Issued Date

For Immediate Release

Title [Be brief, attention-grabbing and unique.]

The first sentence [Summarise the story. Get the key points across to catch the journalist's attention. Answer who, what, where, when, why and how.]

Second paragraph [Explanation. Sell yourself here; what is unique or new about your story? Write in the present tense, and use 'he' or 'she' instead of 'I'. If you have any statistics add them here. Illustrate your story with quotes. A quote, written in italics, from a key person, helps bring a story to life. Make sure your quote adds new information to the release.]

[Use low resolution photos or logos to catch the journalist's eye.]

[Finish off with an overview – such as dates, times, how to order or contact you – these should be the details you'd like to see in print.]

##Ends##

Notes to editors

1. Contact details – [include mobile, landline and email if possible, company name, and website address].

2. Images – [state whether you have high resolution images available and/or are available to have your photo taken].

3. Background info – [include a summary of background information: when the company was launched, any achievements, mini biography of the founder, etc].

SOCIAL MEDIA

Marketing via social media enables you to develop an online community talking about you and your products. See every encounter as a new opportunity and grab it.

I write a detailed business blog (**www.joannedewberry.co.uk**) about how I promote and develop brand awareness for Charlie Moo's via social media. I also now use it to promote myself, for example, I wrote about writing this book! Social media acted as a great forum to ask questions, gather information and seek out case studies and is, essentially, when used correctly, *free* PR and marketing, which is See every encounter as a new opportunity and grab it." crucial in developing awareness for the small business. It really can be a make or break solution, especially if your budget is limited.

Social media is a fun and interactive way to promote yourself. There are a variety of different platforms for all kinds of people – even the shy! When I first started Charlie Moo's, I was (and still am) primarily a full-time mum. Although I now have three children, my primary goals remain the same. Time is of the essence, and sometimes face-to-face networking is not the easiest option for business mums, people in employment and/or those based in rural villages. Breakfast meetings? Who on earth wants to babysit my children at 7am?! But if I go online while the children are happily eating their breakfast there is an infinite number and variety of small business owners looking to network.

Social networking not only enables you to tap into your target market, interact and make connections with other businesses, it is also a great learning tool. Through social networking I have developed a greater knowledge and understanding of various aspects of business development and my confidence has grown.

But it is no good just joining, say, Facebook, creating a business page and sitting back. You need to update it every day and interact with your fans/likers who are your potential and possibly repeat customers. This in itself can be time-consuming and you can get easily sidetracked, so allocate yourself a time limit, e.g. 15 minutes per working day.

Remember that although social media provides you with a broad range of potential customers, business mentors, networking opportunities and people you would never normally meet or interact with, it does have drawbacks and potential dangers. Whether it's third parties writing about you, your products or the way in which you represent yourself, be aware of how you come across when responding. Social media enables your customers to find out exactly what kind of person you are, and your history, so make sure everything they see is professional, helpful and honest.

Pros

- It's FREE!

- A great way to connect with your target audience

- Raises brand awareness

- A great tool for building partnerships and supporting other businesses by mentioning and linking to them

- Useful for networking with other small businesses outside of your local community

- An easy and friendly way to engage with customers and conduct online market research

Cons

- Can be time-consuming and distracting, so plan your time effectively

- You cannot control what other people say – good or bad – but you can respond

- Beware of getting too personal with your followers – remember, they are potential customers not friends

Log off

Turn off your social media channels when you're not using them. It's too easy to be distracted by new messages, friends and conversations when you're trying to get things done.

Although there is a wide abundance of social media platforms, I have chosen to concentrate on three: Facebook pages, Twitter and blogging. I have had continued success with these channels, know how they work and have included my top tips.

FACEBOOK PAGE

Facebook fans are 41% more likely to recommend a brand and 28% more likely to continue using them. Fans spend an average $71.84 (£44.26) more than non-fans and are worth about $136.38 (£84.06)*. Which brand wouldn't want a Facebook fan strategy and to grow their Facebook army?

Facebook has developed into a great way to advertise your business. Small businesses have been using it for years and now large corporates are directing consumers to their Facebook pages rather than their own websites. Advertisers have cottoned on to the fact that Facebook has become key in communication. Every time you as an individual 'like' pages anywhere on the web it appears on your personal Facebook profile which then appears on your friends' feeds. This is a goldmine; the potential amount of customers you could reach without even trying is immense. If Facebook was a country it would be the third largest in the world in terms of population.

WARNING

Facebook does not allow you to have more than one profile and you are not permitted to have a profile page as your business. You personally must have a profile and from there you can set up a business Page (Groups aren't designed to promote businesses either).

---

*(www.barnraisersllc.com/2011/08/roi-walmarts-facebook-page-lot-measure)

How to set up a page

Go to your personal profile (you'll need to set up a basic record if you don't have one already), scroll down to the very bottom and click on 'Create a Page'.

Six options will be visible:

1. Local business or place

2. Company, organisation or institution

3. Brand or product

4. Artist, band or public figure

5. Entertainment

6. Cause or community

Click on 'Local business or place' and select the category which best describes you (I would suggest either Local Business or Shopping/Retail), and then it's just a case of filling in the blanks.

Ensure that you claim your vanity URL (**www.facebook.com/yourusername**) as this snappier version will be easier to add (and remember) on other resources, such as Twitter, your email signature and business cards. Just select 'Manage' then 'Edit page', click on 'Basic Information' and select Username. Charlie Moo's' is **www.facebook.com/charliemoos.fanpage**.

Tips

- Don't get hooked on (or brag about) the number of likes/fans you have. Having 1,000 is great but if only a small proportion of them interact with your page – i.e. comment or like your status updates, photographs, links, etc. and ultimately buy your products – then the other 900 are irrelevant.

- The key is quality not quantity in terms of fans, posts and interactions.

- Sort the images that you upload into albums. It's very simple feature but it's underused by businesses. It will help potential customers find what they are looking for (and maybe even something they weren't).

- Check your Insights on a regular basis. Similar to Google Analytics these show you where people have come from (e.g. Twitter, Facebook, a blog, your website, etc.), which posts have been the most popular and how many of your followers/fans interact with you. Use this information to focus your energies on the media that works best for you.

My business would not be where it is today without Facebook; it has been a godsend. I use it to reach new customers, let people know what Charlie Moo's has been doing, flag my award nominations, promote new products and list my media coverage (with accompanying images/scans). Facebook pages are brilliant, easy to use and a great way to communicate and interact with a lot of people in a variety of ways. I am frequently asked how to encourage interaction (it is *social* media after all), so here are my top tips:

- Post questions – everyone has an opinion!

- Write topical updates about your business or relevant current affairs

- Reply to your fans' comments.

- Post videos – perhaps of an event you attended or a simple craft activity.

- Post links to relevant websites (including your own).

- Post images – I sometimes upload images of fabric and ask people's opinion.

In a world where we are reliant on networking and word of mouth, you will of course meet people who want to 'be your friend' on Facebook. My personal profile reflects my life. It's full of information, news and pictures of my children, family, and friends both old and new. I have done this consciously, so I am careful about my language, put privacy settings on photos and remove anything unsavoury from my younger days. Remember that your personal life could reflect on your business reputation. If you don't want networking acquaintances to be Facebook friends (and see your personal profile) direct them to your page and encourage them to interact with you there.

I know many small businesses who actually sell all their products through a Facebook page – all you need is an organised ordering system, a way to take payments (PayPal is probably best and easiest), but most importantly you need a fanbase.

Laura Renton started her business That's Sew Laura (**www.thatssewlaura.co.uk**) after posting pictures of clothes she had made for her daughter on her profile. She soon sold a few pieces to friends and then their friends saw them:

> "I started to get contacted via my personal profile. I decided I wanted to keep everything separate, so setting up a Facebook page seemed like the most logical step."

Selling products via Facebook

There are a variety of ways you can sell via Facebook, with the simplest being to set up albums of images with descriptions and prices.

> "I didn't know how else to advertise my cupcakes without spending a fortune so I thought Facebook was the best place to start. I started by posting on my wall the occasions I was making for (my first being a Valentine's cupcake delivered to your home, workplace, etc.). People emailed me or private messaged me with their order. They either paid in advance with PayPal or cash on delivery. I had two orders on the very first day and would have been happy with ten but I ended up having 30 orders!"
>
> **– Natalie Pike (www.haveyourcakeandiceit.co.uk)**

"I make up samples of each design, then have an online album which contains all of the fabrics customers can choose from. People can select which design they would like, and then which fabric. In addition, last autumn I held a ready-made sale on my Facebook page to sell stock I had left from events throughout the summer. It went amazingly well and I now plan to make ready-made items for the new winter collection, along side taking my usual bespoke orders."

– Laura Renton (www.thatssewlaura.co.uk)

Laura uses PayPal for invoicing as it the most effective method for her. If the customer does not have a PayPal account then they can still pay into Laura's by using a credit/debit card. It is one of the most secure ways to transact, as no card or account details are given to the retailer. The seller does, however, have to pay merchant fees which at the time of writing are 3.4% + £0.20 per transaction on all purchases under £1,500.

You can also add a 'contact me' application, which can double up as an order form. This is particularly useful if you make personalised items as you can gather and keep all the information you need in one place.

Applications are easy to add to your page and all come with their own supporting page and/or website. Payvment (**www.payvment.com**) is the most popular, probably because there are no fees, no listing fees and no set-up fees. You do still have PayPal fees but the customer does not leave the Facebook site. (Applications like Etsy and Folksy will take your customer to their own site.)

Getting your website (whether selling direct or through a third party) in front of other people is an art form in itself and one of the key aspects of Facebook is the sharing mechanism. For example, I 'like' something so it appears in my feed, therefore all my friends see it and inevitably some will like it too. This is what drives more people – potential customers – to your page.

"Facebook just seems to work for me. I can interact well with customers and they seem to like that. After posting on Facebook I made sales pretty much instantly. I was quite shocked how quickly everything happened. Sewing went from being a hobby, to a part-time job, to a 'sewing for 6-8 hours per day' job, which I really wasn't expecting. People wanting to buy things from me? What a lovely surprise!!"

– Laura Renton (www.thatssewlaura.co.uk)

"No matter where else I advertise and how much I pay out, Facebook has been the best at generating income for me!"

– Natalie Pike (www.haveyourcakeandiceit.co.uk)

TWITTER

Twitter, the social networking and micro-blogging service, launched in 2006. It enables users to send and read messages called tweets. These are text-based posts of up to 140 characters which are displayed on the user's profile page. Users can follow each other, forward (or retweet) other people's messages and easily reply and respond to each other.

67% of Twitter users are more likely to buy from the brands they follow.* Twitter is growing fast because it's instant, interactive and puts you in direct touch with people you never dreamed you could reach. I use Twitter mainly for PR and self-promotion and try not to get caught up in the social side of it. What works best for me is the real-time aspect. I tweet and receive replies straightaway from a variety of people giving me a cornucopia of information, wealth and knowledge. I find what I'm looking for quicker than a Google search or a flick through Yellow Pages.

---

* Essential Twitter stats data
(**blog.hubspot.com/blog/tabid/6307/bid/12234/10-Essential-Twitter-Stats-Data.aspx**)

Twitter is a great resource, as long as you're following the right people. You do not have to follow everyone who follows you – again, it's quality not quantity. If you are using Twitter to increase your PR profile, then make sure you are following the magazines, websites and newspapers relevant to your business, as they always tweet upcoming features, case studies and products they are looking for. Hopefully they will follow you in return, read your tweets and you'll gain some media coverage.

Don't just tell people about your business – think talking *to* not talking *at*. Interact and engage with your followers and the people you follow, take an interest in what they are doing and respond. Again, be aware that these mediums require 100% transparency and you have to ensure that you are sending out the right message. Your language and dialogue will influence people's perception and opinion of you and your brand.

How to set up and use Twitter

1. Go to **www.twitter.com** and complete the short sign-up form.

2. You will then be asked for your prefered username. It is best to use your business name or as close to it as possible. Your direct URL will then be **twitter.com/yourbusinessname** (mine is **twitter.com/charliemoos** or **@charliemoos** for short).

3. Once logged in you will see a status box where you can write your 140 character update (Compose new Tweet...). You will also see a head and shoulders icon in the top right-hand corner'. Select Settings from the dropdown menu and then add a picture or logo, description, URL, etc. It is important to do this to give authenticity to your account, and so that people can find you.

Tweet management

Using a free platform like TweetDeck (**www.tweetdeck.com**) or HootSuite (**www.hootsuite.com**) will make Twitter easier to use and more manageable, e.g. you can easily run multiple accounts and schedule in Tweets to be sent at a later date.

Lingo

● Tweet – The 140-character message you write.

● RT/Retweet – Sending another person's update to your followers (similar to forwarding an email).

● @USERNAME – Simply start a message with @username of the person you want to connect to in your update. Only people following you and that person will be able to see it though. If you want everyone to then add a full stop, other symbol, or 'Hi' before their name, for example .@charliemoos or Hi @charliemoos.

● DM/Direct Message – These are private messages between you and the recipient (a bit like email). You have to be following each other in order to send a DM.

● Hashtag # – People create hashtags to summarise what a tweet is about, then when somebody searches for that hashtag, they will find all the related messages.

The real-time aspect of Twitter makes it a popular tool with television and radio programmes. Daytime magazine-style shows such as ITV's *This Morning* encourage viewers to respond to various topics via Twitter (and also their Facebook page). You can either send a tweet to @nameofshow and/or include the hashtag they mention. The presenters can then read out and discuss the comments being made during the live show. The BBC's political programme *Question Time* uses the hashtag #bbcqt and you can follow viewers' responses to the topics as they are being discussed live in the studio. Genius use of social media if you have a readymade audience, but how can you as a small business make it work for you?

It's simple – just start your own hashtag relevant to your business.

Mumpreneur UK (**www.mumpreneuruk.com**) have #mumpreneurhour everyday at 2pm discussing business issues that matter to mums in business.

Multimillionaire business guru Theo Phaphitis (*Dragons' Den*) has #SBS – Small Business Sunday – whereby small business owners send a 140 character message ending in #SBS between 5pm and 7:30pm on a Sunday evening and the 6 'winners' are re-tweeted by Theo. Here are a few examples:

> @babysigningmum – #SBS I facilitate communication between parents and babies, through classes, training, making baby signing accessible to all. @theophaphitis (October 2010)

> @sinceritygifts – #SBS Unique, Organic, Eco-Friendly, Gorgeous Gifts and Homewares for all occasions www.sinceritygifts.co.uk @theophaphitis (April 2011)

> @charliemoos – #SBSudderly mooverlous business mummy 3under 5's designer/crafter www.charliemoos.co.uk business blogger www.joannedewberry.co.uk @TheoPaphitis (February 2012)

OK, my tweet wasn't a mere 140 characters but I use Tweetdeck which minimises URLs thereby freeing up characters (Twitter has now added this function too).

Hashtags are also a great way to join in or follow a conversation or gauge the opinion of the masses, for example, #xfactor is always a popular hashtag. You can monitor what's trending on Twitter (based on hashtags and tweet contents) by country or worldwide.

Tips

- Follow people relevant to your business. Don't follow everyone otherwise you will waste time sifting through irrelevant information, fun though it may be.

- Interact with other people's tweets and don't tweet too much about your business, otherwise you will look spammy and people won't be interested.

- Link to your website from your tweets and add your Twitter feed to your site, making it easy for people to become followers.

- Link your Facebook page and/or blog to your Twitter account and this will automatically post your Facebook status and blog content onto Twitter. It's efficient and might reach different people.

TweetDeck

- TweetDeck (**www.tweetdeck.com**) allows you to organise your followers, mentions, DMs and #hashtags in neat columns, making it easier to keep track.

- Every so often a pop-up will appear in the righthand corner of your screen, letting you know if you have any mentions, DMs or #hashtags.

- TweetDeck enables you to run more than one Twitter account side-by-side, e.g. you might have a personal and business account.

Twitter PR Tips

- Make a clear distinction between working and socialising on Twitter and try to limit your usage, otherwise it's easy to lose hours that should have been spent crafting.

- Make sure you're following local magazines, radio stations and newspapers, as they will all be on Twitter looking for local news.

- Find out if national magazines, papers, etc. are online. Many of the glossies use Twitter to find case studies or products for stories/features they have coming up.

- Search for #journorequest and see if you can help. If you do end up in contact with a journalist then make sure you save their email into your media database.

Social media bookmarking

Social networking sites such as Facebook and Twitter are not just for socialising; we all love to share information, videos, products we like, you name it we share it! By adding social media bookmarks to your site you enable others to easily share your page, photos, etc. on their Facebook and Twitter feeds. If they have 200+ friends then your business has now reached another 200 potential customers, for FREE and with no extra work to you.

The easiest one to use is **www.addthis.com**. You can customise the size, colours and platforms it shares then just add the HTML code provided when and where you require it.

BLOG

According to Blogger (**www.blogger.com**) one of the leading blog platforms:

> "A blog is a personal diary. A daily pulpit. A collaborative space. A political soapbox. A breaking-news outlet. A collection of links. Your own private thoughts. Memos to the world.
>
> Your blog is whatever you want it to be. There are millions of them, in all shapes and sizes, and there are no real rules.
>
> In simple terms, a blog is a website where you write stuff on an ongoing basis. New stuff shows up at the top, so your visitors can read what's new. Then they comment on it or link to it or email you. Or not."

Well, I think that covers everything.

Why have a blog?

A blog enables you to:

● build relationships with potential customers

● build your brand awareness

● develop an email list/customer database

● develop SEO (search engine optimisation) – if you are keeping your content fresh, new and relevant, you should come higher in the search ranks.

What value will a blog give your business?

That really depends on you. A blog takes dedication but if you can keep it going, gain lots of readers, Facebook likes, Re-tweets and commenting, then you can build up your own community. The main reason blogs fail is a lack of content. You need to blog regularly and use the space as a PR campaign. Build relationships with your readers. Be human and show interest. It is an opportunity to really show off your expertise and knowledge as you can write far more than you would on Facebook, and certainly Twitter! Sell yourself as an expert in your area and you may become sought-after.

 Give your business some personality and show off your skills."

Blogs are particularly popular with craft businesses as you have far greater freedom with the design and content than on Facebook and Twitter, which you can use to direct people to your blog. You could even set up a vlog, or video blog. Give your business some personality and show off your skills.

Blog platforms

- **Blogger (www.blogger.com)** – Owned by Google this is a free platform that's great for beginners. However, the design is limited and you don't actually own the blog so at any point (not that this happens very often) Blogger can just shut you down. You can transfer your Blogger to WordPress in due course if you wish.

- **WordPress.com** – The .com version is free and easy to set up. A great benefit is that set-up, upgrades, spam, security, etc. are all taken care of, and everything is backed up automatically. However, you cannot customise the themes, display adverts or make money from sponsored advertising. The WordPress plugins (nifty add-ons that extend the ability of apps/software) are not compatible either.

- **WordPress.org** – The admin section of the .org version looks the same as the .com one, but this platform allows you to have full control of the templates and design, and you can install plugins, or even do some coding (if you are technically minded). You are required to backup your system yourself and perform manual upgrades, but neither of these are difficult. You also have to pay a hosting fee which varies considerably, from

£14.99 a year to over £50. It depends on the bandwidth you use, the amount of memory you need, the number of hits your blog receives, etc.

- **Blogs attached to websites** – Many websites come with their own blogging facility, and these are fine to use but be aware that they may not always be compatible with software designed for platforms such as Blogger and WordPress. The blog I use for Charlie Moo's is powered by Create, my website provider, but it's incompatible with Technorati, the blog-specific search engine

If you're unsure about investing money in your blog, start with Blogger or WordPress.com. You can always transfer your content over later to WordPress.org.

How else can you make a blog work for you?

Plan your blog posts for the month and write and schedule in as many as possible in advance. This frees you up to deal with real-time issues such as taking orders, making products, going to fairs and social networking.

Here are a few writing tips:

- Aim to post a minimum of one article a week. I personally post three, but it depends on the time you have available and the number of topics you can cover.

- Make a list of the topics for the amount of posts you plan to write.

- Write notes for each topic or, if you can, jump straight in and write 200-400 words about it.

- If your blog platform doesn't allow you to schedule posts through its system, then write them as Word documents or draft emails, and plan the dates (and time) you are going to post them. In terms of timing, weekends aren't ideal, neither is after 3pm or days that you are out, perhaps at a craft fair (but don't forget to blog about that before and after). If you do write at the same time every week, then your regular readers will begin to expect that, so try to be consistent.

- If you're not writing purely about business then decide whether you want to include any personal information (your children's names, marital info, details about your life, etc.). Try to keep it consistent either way.

- Use lots of keywords on your blog and link from it to your main website, social media channels, etc.

These are very general tips, so if something happens to you, your business or there's something topical in the news, then run with it and blow the schedule. It's better to post lots than nothing at all.

You will *need* to schedule blogging in and make it part of your routine. Having a list of topics is a good starting point and will ensure you are not staring at a blank screen with half an hour of unexpected spare time thinking '*hmmm, what to write?*' As with social media, it's all about engaging with people and developing relationships. Customers will enjoy seeing/reading what you have been doing – events, news, projects you have been working on and some general life musings, if you fancy it. People buy products and services from people/companies they like, conversely they won't buy from from people they dislike. So be like-able.

Don't think about blogging as a chore. Remember what it will add to your website in terms of traffic, interest, interaction with potential customers and hopefully generating more business.

YouTube

YouTube is also a great way to show off your expertise, and video demonstrations are always sought-after. In the beginning you may have used videos for research, training and inspiration, and now you can be the person new crafters turn to.

You don't even need a super posh camera (but if you can then get or borrow an HD one, as the images are clearer). As with taking photographs, use a tripod to stop any shaking. I use a free piece of software called Windows Movie Maker to edit my videos. You can check out my video blogs, testimonials, how to's and how not to's at **www.youtube.com/user/joannedewberry/videos**.

CONCLUSION

It was no surprise that the crafters I spoke to all use social media and most blog regularly. Viv Smith (**www.poppysparkles.co.uk**) uses Facebook, Twitter and writes a blog:

> "I've run one competition on my blog and am about to launch another. I am also getting active in the teams on Etsy and am setting up the social media for the British Sellers on Etsy team (@BritishEtsyTeam). With two young children it's been hard to do promotion other than online and leaving business cards in various local venues."

Getting to know your audience and being 'real' and personable is a great way to engage with your customers. People will always buy from people, make sure that person is you! Here is a top tip from Darren Toms (**www.darrentoms.com**), a leadership coach:

> "Social media is a great tool for you and your business BUT, like all tools, it needs to be used in the right way to make it effective. A hammer is a great tool for banging nails into a wall…but you don't use a hammer to fix a window.

> Use social media carefully and effectively to manage your reputation and influence your fans and followers to say great things about you and your business."

You can learn all the tricks of the trade for Facebook, Twitter, blogging, etc. but personal preference will always prevail. Never worry about what everyone is doing. Try something, and if you don't like it or find it useful then try something else. Marketing is a valuable asset, but if your time is being wasted then you will ultimately fail. Be brave enough to steer your business in the correct direction.

ACTIVITY #6:
GRANNY HARRIS'S EVERYDAY MARMALADE

by Parkside Produce

This is my Great Great Grandmother's recipe and it makes about 7lb/3kg.

You will need

- 2lb Seville oranges (juiced, pips collected, remaining skins minced)

- 1–2 lemons, depending on their size (juiced, pips collected, remaining skins minced)

- 4 pints water

- 4lb granulated sugar

Useful starting points

(If you know roughly what you are doing feel free to move on and ignore this bit!)

- Make sure your pan is big enough. When the marmalade reaches a rolling boil it will rise up the pan – three to four times the volume. If it boils over it makes a MESS!

⦿ Do you know how to test for a set? Read the instructions on page 127 if you are not sure.

⦿ Make sure your spoon has a long enough handle – you don't want to lose it in the hot marmalade, and you want to have your hands as far from the boiling, sticky mass as possible!

⦿ Make sure you have the heat turned DOWN when you add the sugar, and wait for it to completely dissolve before turning the heat back up. If the sugar burns, the marmalade is ruined. You will feel (using the spoon) that the sugar has all dissolved as it won't be gritty on the bottom of the pan.

⦿ Have enough jars (and lids that fit correctly) washed, dry and warming in the oven. We don't have a dishwasher, so ours get a soapy wash, rinsed, then dried at 140°C. The jars are sterilised and just the right temperature for the marmalade; not too hot for the marmalade to bubble up in the jar, but hot enough not to crack when the hot marmalade is added.

⦿ If you are using wax discs have these ready.

⦿ A jam funnel and a heatproof jug that pours nicely are also useful for transferring the hot marmalade to the jam jars. These should also be washed and dried before use.

⦿ Make sure you give yourself plenty of time, as this is not a job to be hurried.

Method

Step 1. Put the minced fruit in the preserving pan with the juice and water. Put the pips into a muslin bag, fold in all the edges (you don't want threads of muslin in your marmalade!) and tie securely to the pan, pushing the bag into the mixture. Leave to soak overnight.

Step 2. The next day, heat the mixture until the volume has reduced by half. We have a spoon that we have marked the depth that needs to be reached, as our pan does not have measurements on the inside. If you have a Maslin pan which has the volume marked on inside then this job is easy! Remove the muslin bag and put it in a sieve over a jug to cool.

Step 3. Add the sugar, and once it has dissolved slowly bring the mixture to the boil. Meanwhile, squeeze the cooled muslin bag to extract all the useful sticky juice and tip this pectin-rich juice back into the pan.

Step 4. Once a rolling boil is reached and the surface looks glassy, test for a set. If you are using a thermometer then 150°c is setting point.

Step 5. Once setting point is reached allow the marmalade to cool for at about ten minutes so the bits don't float to the top.

Step 6. Pot the hot marmalade into warm sterilised jars and seal. Fill the jar to the neck, where the jar bends and meets the screw thread.

Step 7. Label your jars once cooled. If you jiggle them about too much when they are still warm the marmalade might seep over the top of the wax disc.

Shelf life – It's about two years, but I doubt it will last that long! It is ready to eat immediately, although I would suggest you wait for it to cool down so that you don't burn your tongue! Your marmalade will improve in flavour if it is left for about a month.

Additions and alterations – You can change the type of sugar used (light brown, dark brown, Muscovado or Demerara), add fresh grated ginger or crushed spices to the muslin bag, add some alcohol, or add fruit pieces to the mixture (crystallised ginger or dried cranberries). I add 1tbsp of alcohol per 1lb of fruit at setting point. This means the alcohol evaporates and leaves the flavour, so add alcohol that you like the taste of! Whisky, Bundaberg rum and Cointreau feature in some of my varieties.

Testing for a set

Put a china saucer (or two) into the coldest part of your fridge, or your freezer, just after you have put your marmalade on to reduce in volume. Once you think your marmalade has reached setting point, turn off the heat. Stir the marmalade and drop a dollop from the spoon onto a cold plate. Put it back into the fridge and wait (impatiently!) for two minutes. When the time is up, bring the saucer out and push the dollop with your finger. If the surface of the marmalade has formed a skin and wrinkles when you push it woo hoo you've made marmalade! If it doesn't, not to worry, just bring the marmalade back to the boil again and keep boiling hard for five minutes, and then test for a set again. This is why it is useful to have more than one saucer prepared!

*   *   *

If all this sounds like far too much hard work, come and taste some of Parkside Produce's (**www.parksideproduce.co.uk**) delicious marmalade selection at our next event. You won't go away empty-handed!

CONCLUSION

 AND

CASE STUDIES

CONCLUSION

All businesses are individual, but particularly so when it comes to crafts. Each business has its own unique requirements, and you should now be equipped with your plan to take your business forward in terms of pricing, selling, branding, marketing, merchandising and PR.

Minor changes = maximum potential. I often liken business to a snowball – you do a bit of this and a bit of that and suddenly you are rolling along at a rate of knots and everything is falling into place and coming together. Just like a snowball, the more you roll, the bigger it gets.

You are now armed with the information and ready to start, but the execution is up to you. Just remember, if something doesn't work first time, don't give up; persevere or try a different approach. I cannot give you any instant solutions to increasing sales or developing a credible brand. It is all up to you. But I hope I have inspired you to go for it. It will take hard work and dedication, but it will all pay dividends in the end.

CASE STUDIES

I'm extremely grateful to all my case studies and in this section you can find out a bit more about them and their businesses.

- Caroline Watts, Caroline Watts Embroidery
- Erica Martyn, Odds and Soxlets
- Nadine Thomas, Nellie Dean
- Viv Smith, Poppy Sparkles
- Laura Renton, That's Sew Laura
- Jamie Fry, Uncle Bundle Crafts
- Andrea Palluch, Skin Bistro

CAROLINE WATTS

Caroline Watts Embroidery

www.carolinewattsembroidery.co.uk

Randomly, I went to sixth form college with Caroline in Yorkshire and we were reunited via Twitter. I admire Caroline's business, which is inspired by vintage French linens. Her products scream high end, premium market and – more importantly – 'buy me!'

Caroline Watts Embroidery is run by a mother and daughter team in rural North Yorkshire. Each product is lovingly hand embroidered by Caroline and carefully finished by her mother, Anne. The finest linen, threads and French lavender are used to create beautiful home accessories for both the traditional and modern home.

Inspirations for embroidery designs come from woodland walks in the beautiful Yorkshire countryside along with the tranquil setting of Caroline's garden and also the embroidery done in the 1940s by Caroline's grandmother.

Our aim is to create something which is not only affordable, but also to be treasured and kept for future generations. We also aim to create something that everybody can afford, that is well made and made in the UK. So many things you see in shops are poor quality, made abroad and very expensive. Handmade should not necessarily be regarded as a luxury, but as an essential. Our aim is to provide products which are a little bit different from the usual; maybe a bit quirky, but overall something that is affordable and beautiful.

Our ethos is very much that of William Morris: "Have nothing in your house that you do not know to be useful, or believe to be beautiful."

We sell a variety of products such as cushions, tea cosies, egg cosies, personalised pictures, lavender hearts and bags through our own website and **notonthehighstreet.com**. We also sell through local craft fairs twice a year.

Caroline's Five Top Tips

1. Follow your dream and believe in yourself.

2. Be prepared for hard work and long days.

3. Make sure you allow for some time off or you'll end up hating your hobby!

4. Join Twitter. It has been a great support for me.

5. Make a Facebook Fan page and start a blog. They are great ways to keep everyone up to date with your business, but make sure you contribute on a regular basis.

ERICA MARTYN

Odds and Soxlets

www.oddsandsoxlets.co.uk

Erica is mum to 1-year-old Harry. She launched her first business, Odd and Soxlets, in April 2011. As a talented artist Erica has lots of ideas for future plans and ventures. I wish her incredible success with her business.

Odds & Soxlets is the quirky home of my sock creations and illustrations. Odds & Soxlets is a small, internet-based company where you will find bespoke hand-crafted soxlets – soft toys made from socks – alongside co-ordinating illustrated handmade cards within our handmade shop. I have a variety of socks in my sock shop; I also take requests for custom orders and can make any clothing for soxlets too. All of my soxlets are carefully made to exceed all safety requirements. Each soxlet is hand-made from a brand-new pair of socks, some of which are odd. All eyes and smiles are hand-embroidered, making them safe for babies and young children, and all of the soxlets are CE marked. I am also currently working with a retailer in Chesterfield to provide my soxlets and co-ordinating cards for their handmade-gift shop.

In our create and craft shop, I have created a digital crafting collection using my illustrations including digital stamps, decoupage and patterned papers. I also have free children's colouring in pages and a free digital design each month for anyone who visits my website. Rather than the more traditional way of crafting, digital crafting is a way of purchasing the artwork to print off at home on whatever medium suits you and as many times as you wish, in order to create endless projects in the comfort of your own home! Digital stamps are line art drawings (black outline) which crafters print off and colour or paint to create a topper for a card. Digital decoupage is a sheet of character layers which the crafter prints out onto card and then cuts out to layer on top of each other to create a 3D card topper. The patterned papers are then also printed off onto paper or card and used as the background of your own handmade card!

Our blog posts twice a week (Tuesdays and Thursdays). On Tuesdays my create and craft design team post project ideas and inspiration using my digital crafting collections, and on Thursdays I personally post about any current soxlets I have made, new products, exciting new free designs and so forth. I also use both Facebook and Twitter for social networking and interlink them both with my blog using networked blogs, which for me is a great

way to communicate with potential customers and get more traffic through to my website! Plus, I have set up a Zazzle shop; this basically allows me to upload my artwork onto their products and I receive a percentage of the sales – there are no fees or set-up costs, so this is great for any small business.

Erica's Five Top Tips

1. Research your market and ensure you have a niche.

2. Working from home can reduce your outlay costs and is great for life/work balance.

3. Bear in mind that working for yourself is hard work, however the rewards are worth it!

4. Make sure you interact with the world outside and get yourself known.

5. Use being a mum to your advantage and don't let it put you off working if you have a dream to follow.

NADINE THOMAS

Nellie Dean

www.nellie-dean.com

Nadine is mum to Edward, aged 6. After deciding juggling childcare and office work was not working for her, she took the plunge to start selling her craft wares. Nellie Dean was her nickname as a child and seemed a good choice for her business.

I make bags, bunting, brooches and other things not beginning with B! Mainly textiles, but also hand-painted chalkboards in different colours, greetings cards with fabric pictures on them and scented teacup candles. Much of what I do is eco-friendly, for example the fabric used on the cards and on the brooches makes use of lots of scraps of fabric and so reduces waste. Also, the teacup candles are made in vintage teacups which otherwise would not be used, languishing at the back of a cupboard somewhere.

Nadine's Five Top Tips

1. Do your research.

2. Start by making items, then give them away and ask for feedback, thereby perfecting your products before launching them to market.

3. You can start slowly and build your business organically, without needing major investment.

4. Be prepared for a lot of very enjoyable but hard work.

5. Just do it!

VIV SMITH

Poppy Sparkles

www.poppysparkles.co.uk

Viv is mum to two children under five and is currently on a career break. She is using the time to develop her own successful small business. As well as creating gorgeous products, Viv is also incredibly talented in branding, PR and marketing. Her ideas and suggestions for this book have definitely opened my eyes.

I make hand-crafted jewellery using sterling silver, Swarovski crystal and semi-precious stones in the main. I aim to create fresh, contemporary, but classic pieces that will last and be treasured. I have also started to create accessories from ribbon, such as brooches and hair accessories.

As well as off-the-peg designs, I also offer a bespoke design service. I sell through my own website, as well as Etsy, Folksy and Kiddiebase.

As a self-funded business, I make use of social media for marketing, and blog as a way to raise my profile, satisfy my love of writing/blogging and also to drive traffic to my website.

Viv's Top Five Tips

1. Gather a supportive network around you.

2. Research the market and find your niche and USP.

3. Accept that as a mum you may have to grow more slowly than you'd like, but growing slowly and organically isn't a bad thing – limited time etc. can make you focus and do the essentials

right, setting up firm foundations for growth and development when you are ready.

4. Don't compete on price – it won't make for a viable business.

5. Take the time to build a strong brand and maintain it – it'll help you keep your prices sustainable.

LAURA RENTON

That's Sew Laura

www.thatssewlaura.co.uk

Laura's daughter Alana, aged one, has been not only the inspiration but the driving force behind That's Sew Laura and if you ever meet her you can tell why; she's so darn cute! As a local business, I have met Laura a number of times. I love her naivety and enthusiasm. She enjoys making products so much that she is unaware how truly successful her business is. That's Sew Laura is definitely a range of children's wear to look out for in the future.

That's Sew Laura officially started in January 2011, with a Facebook page. I never thought it would grow so quickly, but it did. I soon had a waiting list of people wanting to order. I now primarily work on bespoke orders for intake-inspired handmade children's clothing and accessories. I started making a few different bits, but have found that I enjoy making the clothing the most, so I now concentrate on this. Customers are able to choose their fabrics, the design they would like and then I make it just for them, often working to custom sizes provided by the customer. I now have a website and have started to go to local events to sell ready-made items.

For bespoke orders I generally have a two-week waiting list most of the time.

Laura's Five Top Tips

1. Don't try too hard – find what you enjoy FIRST!

2. Join an online forum to chat to other mums in business.

3. Attend local networking events – it's great to know you're not alone

4. Facebook can be amazing, if used right.

5. Think about what you're putting out there, and remain professional at all times.

JAMIE FRY

Uncle Bundle

www.unclebundle.com

Jamie Fry is, wait for it … a man! I hunted high and low and found a crafting gentleman in Poole. Jamie has three children and also continues to work a full-time job.

I pride myself in making high quality, handcrafted cards and have now migrated into other quirky jewellery items, such as cufflinks, rings, brooches, key rings, bracelets and necklaces using Lego, Scrabble, dice and buttons amongst other items. My cufflinks are very popular, followed by the button brooches. A shop in Wareham stocks both and they have them on display for sale in store.

A fun use of Scrabble is turning the letters into functional door signs such as open, closed, ladies, gents and various other toilet/door-related signage.

I also make fridge magnets, bookmarks, Fimo light pulls, purses and toys made from felt among other fabrics. From time to time I will sell crafting items as well.

I sell my wares from home, via family and friends, through Facebook and eBay but mainly on the Folksy website, and will attend the odd fete or craft fair if time allows. I have built up enough stock to command the use of a couple of tables.

On request, I will make items to order if someone wants a more special and personal card made or if they want a particular colour of something I have made, like a bracelet.

Jamie's Top Five Tips

1. Plan – How many, how much, what do you need?

2. Research – Who else is doing the same, have you got a USP?

3. Get feedback – Does it work, is it something people want?

4. Advertise – Take up free advertising, join social media sites.

5. Never give up – Even when sales are down or something doesn't work out.

ANDREA PALLUCH

Skin Bistro

www.skinbistro.co.uk

I discovered Andrea via Facebook. She is super talented and her soaps are lovely! Moving from Brazil to London played havoc with her skin which was the driving force (plus her degree in Biology) to learn more about skin creams and how to make them naturally.

I make natural skincare products from scratch in my kitchen, using the highest quality organic and fair-trade ingredients.

My award-winning soap, which is also my bestselling product, is made of organic, extra-virgin olive oil and is loved by mothers and babies and those with sensitive or dry skin conditions.

My facial serums and body balms are sought after for their therapeutic benefits.

I don't use parabens, sulphates, synthetic fragrances, artificial colours, petrochemicals, mineral oils, etc. In fact, it's much easier to tell my clients every single ingredient that goes into my products. There's hardly anything on the label that they wouldn't be able to recognise. Also, every single ingredient is added for a reason, so that your skin can reap the benefits.

I am constantly researching new ingredients, trying new blends and developing new products. I also offer a completely bespoke service, developing products for an individual client, after a consultation, to fulfil their skin needs.

As an award-winning responsible business, I have reduced packaging to a minimum. Soap labels are printed in 100% post-consumer recycled paper. Most other products are sold in glass, and refills in compostible, sustainably-sourced bioplastic are now available. Seasonal gifts are sold in paper boxes or fabric bags without printed branding so that they can be re-used by clients as they wish. I re-use all packaging materials in which raw ingredients and containers come in. I recycle everything I possibly can.

My vision is to become internationally distinguished for cosmetic care excellence. My mission is to nurture skin for life, adjusting formulations to maintain the skin's health. Integrity, accomplishment and perfection are the trinity of values that best describe my practice.

Andrea's Five Top Tips

1. Have a vision and focus.

2. Know your niche market.

3. Test your product – does it sell for a profitable price?

4. Know your limitations and get help, both to kick off and grow.

5. Be persistent but also flexible.

BRANDING

Special thanks go to the following businesses who also answered many an email question for me:

- Darren Toms – **www.darrentoms.com**
- Duffle Bobble – **dufflebobble.blogspot.co.uk**
- Sarah Smith – **www.silverbirchcrafts.co.uk**
- Natalie Pike – **www.haveyourcakeandiceit.co.uk**
- Emma Ringer – **www.EyeSpyBaby.co.uk**
- Elizabeth Geldart – **www.chiggs.co.uk**
- Michelle Williams – **www.thecraftecademy.co.uk**
- Anna Dakin – **www.alohaphotography.co.uk**

Rose Glendinning

(**www.nappybliss.co.uk**)

Who am I?

Mother of one. Passionate about the environment and helping parents make the right decision for them and their babies.

What image do I want to portray?

Professional and knowledgeable with a bit of the hippy at heart.

What do I want to deliver?

Quality, evidenced-based advice and service to parents.

Who is my target market?

Socially aware, educated 'Waitrose mums' as well as those trying to save money. My ideal client? First-time parents with a good social network and green daycare nurseries. What drives them? Doing the right thing for their child, the environment and their finances. What are their aspirations? Doing the right thing for their child's future. For nurseries, it's those who want to differentiate themselves from their competitors. What are their needs? All of the above plus well-timed, good advice.

What makes me special?

Personal knowledge and experience. What's my USP? Individualised advice with on-going support and nappy laundry. What is my niche? Very few nappy laundries are in operation.

What is my business personality?

Professional but open and friendly. No high-pressure sales.

Who are my competition?

Online shops and self-employed nappy advisors. Large disposable nappy manufacturers.

What is my strapline?

"Heaven for baby and earth." It follows on from Nappy Bliss – bliss giving the impression of heavenly, comfortable, enjoyable – so good for both the environment (earth) and baby.

Lorraine Allman

(**www.speedmentorcentral.co.uk**)

Who am I?

I am Lorraine Allman, entrepreneur, researcher and managing director of Speed Mentor Central Limited.

What image do I want to portray?

We wish to portray ourselves as a professional company, firmly focused on the needs of our client groups.

What do I want to deliver?

An opportunity for our clients to build a better business through developing their skills, attitudes and knowledge base. Short, timely interventions of coaching and mentoring which meet the needs of, and have an immediate positive impact on, the individual and their business.

Who is my target market?

I have two target markets. The first group are aspiring or trading entrepreneurs and small businesses. It doesn't matter what type of business they have or are thinking of launching, or at what stage the business is at, but it does help if they are open to the learning and development process about both themselves and their business. Whilst entrepreneurs and small businesses are not a homogeneous group, I think it's fair to say they aspire to succeed in business, although how 'success' looks may be different for different people. For example, some may see success as simply earning enough to make a good living from their business, whereas for others success will be achieved when they have made a significant impact in their industry or have grown the business sufficiently to consider an exit. Again, their needs will vary but they will be looking for support through coaching and mentoring which will have a tangible effect on their bottom line, but which does not require a significant time and financial commitment.

The second target group is professional business coaches and mentors. They will have been involved in coaching and mentoring for some time and are driven by the desire to support entrepreneurs and help small businesses flourish and thrive. I think most professional coaches and mentors do their work because they want to share the experiences and skills they have with others and genuinely want to support and encourage people in business. Their main needs are being able to have channels through which they can reach their target groups easily and also have access to support which enables them to both reflect on their role as coach or mentor, and to undertake a process of continuing development for themselves.

What makes me special?

What makes my company special and our USP is the fact that we offer affordable, short-term professional coaching and mentoring, rather than the traditional approach taken by other organisations. We want people to experience and evaluate the benefits of professional coaching and mentoring without significant time and financial commitments. We also specialise in speed mentoring events to be launched across the UK, focusing on particular entrepreneurial groups and industries.

What is my business personality?

The personality of the business is professional, focused, and client-led. Ways to ensure this comes across to potential customers is through the appearance, navigation and content of the website, company logo, and consistency across all aspects of our interaction with potential clients such as social media, marketing materials and face-to-face contact.

Who are my competition?

There are no other companies offering speed mentoring in the way we do and although there are other 'directories' of business coaches and mentors, these are not combined into a business site with content to support both coach/mentor and clients. Competitors such as professional mentoring organisations usually require the client to commit to significant time and financial commitments.

What is my strapline?

Our company name is Speed Mentor Central and we have a strapline "an online centre of business expertise". Although 'business expertise' is fairly broad we are happy with that as it reflects the professional nature of the business and combined with the company name feel that it gives a clear message about who we are – the central hub of speed mentoring.

RESOURCES

CE Marking

In July 2011 the law regarding children's toys and CE marking changed and the new Toy Safety Directive 2011 came into force. This means that all products designed or intended (whether or not exclusively) for use in play by children under the age of 14 are required by law to have a CE logo.

This includes handmade products that also look like toys even if you have specified they are are for decorative purposes and not suitable for those under the age of 14 years. The only exception to this is Christmas/novelty products which you can find out more about from Trading Standards.

The following websites are really useful to find out specific information:

- **tinyurl.com/craftingCEMark**
- **tinyurl.com/craftingCEMark2**

Food Safety

When selling food products you must ensure that you have undertaken Basic Food Hygiene and your kitchen is properly inspected and certificated.

Contact your Local Council and Environmental Health Authority.

- **www.food.gov.uk**
- **www.hse.gov.uk/lau**

ABOUT BRIGHTWORD PUBLISHING

Brightword publishing is the small business imprint from Harriman House and Enterprise Nation. Brightword produces print books, kits and digital products aimed at a small business and start-up audience, providing high quality information from high profile experts in an accessible and approachable way.

Other books from Brightword

Go Global: How to Take Your Business to the World

By Emma Jones
Print ISBN: 978-1-90800-300-3
eBook ISBN: 978-1-90800-303-4

Selling for Small Business

By Jackie Wade
eBook ISBN: 978-1-90800-308-9
Print ISBN: 978-1-908003-19-5

Finance for Small Business

By Emily Coltman
eBook ISBN: 978-1-90800-306-5
Print ISBN: 978-1-908003-20-1

Motivating Business Mums

By Debbie O'Connor
eBook ISBN: 978-1-90800-309-6